AZ

GAMES
for Everybody

GAMES
for Everybody

MAY C. HOFMAN

TEMPUS

First published 1905
This edition first published 2007

Tempus Publishing
Cirencester Road, Chalford
Stroud, Gloucestershire, GL6 8PE
www.tempus-publishing.com

Tempus Publishing is an imprint of NPI Media Group

British Library Cataloguing in Publication Data.
A catalogue record for this book is available from the British Library.

ISBN 978 0 7524 4346 1

Typesetting and origination by NPI Media Group
Printed and bound in Great Britain

Contents

Foreword

Everyone is fond of having a good time when invited out to a party or social. Sometimes a stupid evening has been spent because either the guests were not congenial or the hostess had not planned good games. The purpose of this book is to furnish just what is needed for a pleasant home gathering, church social, or any other indoor occasion.

Very few, if any, of these games require much preparation. Just use what is in the house, follow the directions given, and a good time will be the result. Some of the games for 'Adults' can be played by the younger ones, and vice versa. Other games, by being changed a little by the hostess, can be made to suit the occasion.

Many of the good old games that everyone has played are here, while the newer ones, which may be strange at first, will prove most enjoyable when everyone has 'caught on', as the saying is.

M.C.H.

PART I

Games for Children

ANIMAL SHOW.

An amusing game for children is one in which each child is to make some sort of animal out of vegetables or fruit, and toothpicks. When all the children have arrived, pass around slips of paper containing a number and the name of some animal. Each one must keep secret what his animal is to be.

Let the hostess prepare a basket of vegetables, potatoes, beets, carrots, and fruits, lemons, bananas, etc., suitable for the occasion, from which the children can take their choice to make their animals. Plenty of toothpicks must be provided for the legs, ears and tails.

Allow five minutes for constructing the creatures.

Then collect the specimens, pinning a number corresponding to the one on the slip, to its back, and arrange the 'show' on a table. Many queer sights will be seen.

The children, having received pencil and paper, should be told to write down the number of each animal, and opposite it what the animal is intended to represent.

A prize can be given to the one who has guessed the greatest number correctly.

CHASE THE RABBIT.

All the children kneel on the floor in a ring with hands on each other's shoulders.

One is chosen to be the 'rabbit' and runs around outside the ring and touches one of the players, who is to chase him to his 'hole'.

The minute the player is touched he must run to the left, while the rabbit goes to the right, must tag the rabbit when they pass each other and try to get back to the 'hole' again. If he fails, he becomes the 'rabbit', and the game goes on as before.

SOAP–BUBBLE CONTEST.

Provide each child with a clay pipe and prepare two basins of soap suds for the game. If a little glycerine is put in the water, the bubbles will last longer.

Divide the company into two sides, an even number in each. Stretch a cord or rope at a medium height across the middle of the room. Two children, one from each side, play at a time. Each stands on his side, blows the bubble from the pipe and blows it toward the opposite side, and over the rope if he can. If it goes over the rope without breaking, he has won one point for his side, if not, his side has lost. Tally is kept as each set plays, and the side that has the most points, wins, and surely deserves a prize.

ROSE GUESS.

Any child can play this simple game. Take a full blown rose and hold it up where all can see it, then let them write on a slip of paper how many petals they think are in the rose.

The petals are then counted by one of the children and the one who guesses the nearest, receives a prize.

Any flower with many petals, can be used.

NEW BLIND MAN'S BLUFF.

The one who is chosen for the 'blind man' does not have his eyes bandaged as in the old game.

Stretch a sheet between two doors and place a light, candle or lamp, on a table some distance from the sheet. The 'blind man' sits on the floor or low chair in front of the light facing the sheet, but he must be so low down that his shadow will not appear on the sheet.

The children form a line and march single file between the light and the 'blind man', who is not allowed to turn around. Thus their shadows are thrown on the sheet and as they pass, the 'blind man' must guess who they are. The children may disguise their walk and height, so as to puzzle him.

As soon as the 'blind man' guesses one correctly, that one takes his place and becomes 'blind man', while the former takes his place in the procession, and the game proceeds as before, but the children had better change places, so the new 'blind man' won't know their positions.

FINDING FLOWERS.

A very simple game for children is one played like the old-fashioned 'London Bridge'.

Two children with joined hands stand opposite each other, and the rest form a ring and pass under the raised hands, while they repeat,

> We're seeking a pansy, a pansy, a pansy,
> We've found one here.

As they say 'here', the raised hands close around the child who was passing by, and 'Pansy' takes the place of the one who caught her, and she names some other flower which is to be found, and the game goes on as before, substituting that flower for pansy.

Then it continues until all the flowers are 'found'.

BEAN–BAG CONTEST.

Prepare an even number of bean bags of moderate size, half of one colour and half of another.

Appoint leaders, who choose the children for their respective sides. There should be an even number on each side. The opponents face each other, with the leader at the head, who has the bag of one colour at his side. The bags are to be passed,

> 1st, with right hand,
> 2nd, with left hand,
> 3rd, with both hands,
> 4th, with right hand over left shoulder,
> 5th, with left hand over right shoulder.

Before the contest begins, it is best to have a trial game, so all understand how to pass the bags.

At a given signal, the leaders begin, and pass the bags as rapidly as possible down the line, observing all the directions. The last one places them on a chair, until all have been passed, and then he sends them back, observing the same rules, until all have reached the leader.

The side who has passed them back to the leader first, and has done so successfully, is the winning side.

BLOWING THE FEATHERS.

The children are seated on the floor, around a sheet or tablecloth. This is held tight by the players about 1½ ft from the floor, and a feather is placed in the middle.

One is chosen to be out, and at a given signal from the leader, the feather is blown from one to the other, high and low, never allowed to rest once.

The player outside runs back and forth, trying to catch the feather. When he does succeed, the person on whom it rested or was nearest to, must take his place.

SCHOOL.

The players sit in a circle, and each takes the name of some article found in the schoolroom, such as desk, rubber, blackboard, etc.

One of the players stands in the centre and spins a plate on end; as he does so, he calls out the name of an article which one of the players has taken.

The person named must jump up and catch the plate before it stops spinning.

If he is too slow, he must pay a forfeit. It is then his turn to spin the plate.

HIDE THE THIMBLE.

All the players but one leave the room. This one hides a thimble in a place not too conspicuous, but yet in plain sight.

Then the others come in and hunt for the thimble; the first one seeing it, sits down and remains perfectly quiet until all the others have found it.

The first one who saw it, takes his turn to hide it.

FAN BALL.

Make two balls, one red and one blue, out of paper thus –

No. 1   No. 2   No. 3

Slip No.1 in No.2, and No.3 fits over and bisects the other two.

Appoint two leaders who choose their teams; each team takes a ball and a palm leaf fan.

Goals – Three chairs, one at each end of the room and one in the centre, at equal distance from others.

Two play at a time, one player from each side. The player stands in front of his goal and at the word 'ready', fans his ball to the opposite goal. It must go through the back of the chair in the middle of the room, and through the opposite goal, in order to win. When all have finished playing, the team which has the most successful players in it, wins the game.

SPOOL FLOWER HUNT.

Gather together as many spools as possible, marking each with a separate letter, which, when put together, will form the name of some flower, such as: rose, violet, daisy, pansy, etc. Stand all the spools in a row, those forming names standing together.

One child, the gardener, gathers up all the spools and hides them in all the corners and out-of-the-way places in the room, only one spool being in each place. When all are hidden, the children are summoned in to hunt for the flowers.

The object is to find such spools as form a name. As the spools are found, the children see if the letters on them spell a flower.

When the hunt is over, the one having the most complete sets of flowers is the winner.

MARBLE CONTEST.

Cut five holes of different sizes in the lid of a pasteboard box. Number the largest hole 5; the next largest 10; the next, 20; the next, 50; and the smallest, 100.

Place the box on the floor and give each child an equal number of marbles. The object of the game is to see which child can count the most by dropping the marbles into the box through the holes.

Each player in turn stands over the box, holds his arm out straight, even with the shoulder, and drops the marbles one by one into the box. If one goes through the largest hole it counts 5, if through the smallest, 100, and so on, count being kept for each player. The one scoring the greatest number of points is the winner.

PASSING BY.

An amusement for children on a train, or at home when it is raining, is the following, and it will help to while away the time.

If there are several children, choose sides and appoint one to keep the count for his side. Each side sits by a different window and watches the passers-by. Every man counts 1; every woman 2; baby 3; animal 5; white horse 10; black cat 50.

As a child sees someone passing, he calls out the number for his side; if a woman, he says 2; if a man and woman together, it will be 3, and so on.

If the children are looking upon the same street the side that calls its number out first adds it to its score. It is more exciting if the different sides have different streets to look out on.

If on a train, one side sits on the right and the other on the left, and when an object is seen, they call out right, 5, or left, as the case may be, for the mother, or older person to put down on the score card.

The side which succeeds in reaching 100 first is the winning side. If the trip is long, 500 can be the limit.

THE SERPENT'S TAIL.

This is a Japanese game, and is played this way. All the children form a line, each resting his hands on the shoulders of the player in front of him. One child is chosen out, and is called the 'catcher'. The first child of the line, or 'serpent', is called the 'head', and the last one, the 'tail'.

The 'catcher' stands about three feet from the 'head' and when someone gives a signal he tries to catch the 'tail' without pushing anyone, or breaking through the line.

The children forming the 'body' defend the 'tail', by moving about in any way they choose, but the line must never be broken, as the 'tail' is considered caught if it is.

When the 'tail' is caught, the 'catcher' becomes 'head', and the 'tail' is then 'catcher', the last child in the line being 'tail', and the game goes on as before.

LITTLE BO–PEEP.

Dress the little girl in whose honour the party is given as Little Bo-Peep, with a little crook.

Hide small toy sheep all over the room in every nook and corner. As each child comes, give her a little stick fixed up like a crook, and tell the children to find the sheep.

After the hunt is over, award the child who found the most sheep some little prize. Each may keep the sheep she finds.

If the party is in honour of a little boy, change it to 'Little Boy Blue', and have horns instead of crooks.

SPOOL ARMIES.

Children may derive a lot of fun from a large supply of empty spools of all shapes and sizes. Pieces of cotton batting stuck in the opening at the top may serve as heads.

For the 'army' gather together as many spools of the same size as you can, numbering each one. Choose a large spool for the general.

Arrange them in rows with the general at the head of a chair or box. A small ball, or pieces of muslin knotted into small balls, will serve as ammunition. When the battle begins, each child aims at the general, endeavouring to knock him over, and as many others as he can. The score is counted after each attack. If a spool has fallen over, but not off the chair, it counts but half its number; if on the floor, it is 'dead', and the whole number is counted.

SPINNING FOR 20.

On a board or piece of cardboard mark with pencil or ink the design illustrated, the size of the circles varying with the size of the board.

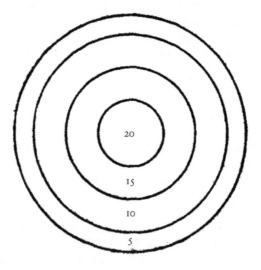

A top may be made out of an empty spool by taking one end of it and sticking a piece of wood, pointed at one end about an inch long, through it. Each spool makes two tops which are spun with the thumb and forefinger. A penny may be used to spin, in fact any small thing that spins will do for a top.

Number the circles as in the diagram. Place the top on the dot in the centre of circle 20 and spin it. The number of the circle the top stops on, is the number scored. If on a line it counts for the circle next to it. If outside the line of circle 5 it counts nothing.

Any number can play and any number, such as 100 or more, may be the score.

SHOE HUNT.

Shoes, four inches long, are cut out of cardboard, from patterns found in catalogues. The pairs are mixed and hidden all over the room, high and low, behind pictures, under mats, etc.

The girl or boy finding the greatest number of shoes that prove to be pairs receives a prize.

To add to the merriment, several pairs of real shoes may be hidden, too, and the children will enjoy hunting for the mates.

HOP–OVER.

Fun for the children is in store when they play this game. All stand in a circle, not too near each other. One player stands in the centre, holding a rope, or stout cord, at the end of which is attached a weight of some kind.

At the word 'ready' the one in the centre whirls the cord rapidly around near the floor. The players, to prevent it from touching their feet, hop over it as it approaches them.

In a short time every one is hopping and a lively time ensues. The one whose feet were touched takes the centre place and endeavours to hit some other player's feet.

BOUQUET.

This is played similarly to 'Stagecoach'. Any number of children can play it. One is chosen out and is called the 'gardener'.

All the children sit in a circle and the 'gardener' gives each one in turn the name of some flower. When all are named the 'gardener' stands in the centre of the circle and tells how he has gone to the woods to gather certain flowers, how he has transplanted them to form a lovely garden, the care he has to take of them, and so on, telling quite a long story and bringing in the names of all the flowers he has given to the children.

As a flower is mentioned, the child who has that name rises, turns around, and sits down again. Anyone who fails to rise when his flower is named must pay a forfeit. When the gardener says something about a bouquet, all the children rise and exchange seats. Then the 'gardener' tries to get a seat, and if he succeeds, the person who has no seat becomes the 'gardener' and the game goes on as before.

MAKING SQUARES.

Make a square or rectangle of dots, as shown below:

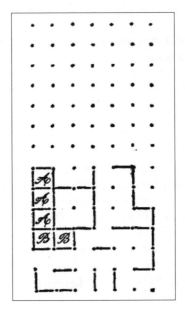

Provide the children with pencils. Each one makes a line joining two dots but tries to prevent the others from making a square.

For a while it is easy, but soon the number of dots is scarce, and it requires careful marking to prevent the squares from being formed. Finally all the chances are gone and the next player completes a square, as a reward he is given another chance, thus completing several, then he joins two dots and the next player continues.

Each one places his initial in his completed square, so the score is easily counted. The one who has succeeded in making the most squares is the winner.

SIMPLE SIMON'S SILLY SMILE.

All the players sit in a circle and one who is bright and witty is chosen as leader. He stands in the centre of the circle and asks the most ridiculous questions he can think of.

The players when asked any question, must always answer 'Simple Simon's silly smile.' No other answer will do and whoever laughs or fails to say it correctly, must pay a forfeit.

TEA-POT.

One player leaves the room, and while he is gone the rest decide upon some word which has several meanings, which he must guess when he comes in.

The rest of the players converse about the word, but instead of mentioning it, say 'tea-pot' in its place. Suppose the word chosen is 'vain'. No.1 may say: 'She is altogether too tea-pot for me', (vain); No.2 says: 'The tea-pot pointed North yesterday', (vane); No.3: 'The tea-pot is blue', (vein), and so on, each in turn making some remark about the chosen word until the player has guessed it correctly. The person who gave the broadest hint about the hidden word must leave the room next.

BLIND-MAN'S BUFF.

It is hardly necessary to describe this game as almost everybody knows how to play it. There may be some who do not know, however, so it is included here.

Clear the room as much as possible, pushing all the chairs, tables, etc., against the walls. The child chosen as 'Buff' is blindfolded, and is asked the following question by the other children. 'How many horses has your father got?' He answers 'Three'. 'What colour are they?' 'Black, white, and grey' is answered. Everyone calls out 'Turn around three times and catch whom you may.'

'Buff' turns around, and then tries to catch whoever he can. The children try to escape him by dodging him until finally one is caught, and before the handkerchief is raised, 'Buff' must guess whom he has caught. If he guesses correctly, the one caught becomes 'Buff'.

CAT AND MOUSE.

The children sit in two rows facing each other, with a space between. Blindfold two children, one being the 'cat' and the other the 'mouse'.

The 'cat' stands at one end of the row and the 'mouse' at the other. They start in opposite directions and the 'cat' tries to catch the 'mouse'. The children may give hints as to the direction the players are to go in. When the 'mouse' is caught, he becomes 'cat', and another child is chosen as 'mouse'.

MUSICAL CHAIRS.

Musical Chairs, or Going to Jerusalem, is a favourite game of the children. Someone who plays the piano well starts up a lively tune and the children march around a row of chairs which have been arranged facing alternately in opposite directions. There should be one less chair than the number of players.

When the music stops, each child tries to find a seat. Someone will be left out, as there is one chair short. This one takes another chair from the row and the game continues until there is one child left with no chair. This one has won the game.

BUTTON, BUTTON.

All the children sit in a circle with hands placed palm to palm in their laps. One child is given a button and she goes to each in turn, slipping her hands between the palms of the children. As she goes around the circle she drops the button into some child's hands, but continues going around as long after as she pleases, so the rest will not know who has it.

Then she stands in the middle of the circle and says: 'Button, button, who has the button?' All the children guess who has it, the one calling out the correct name first is out and it is his turn to go around with the button.

STATUES.

Arrange all the children except one on chairs or a bench. This one is the leader and she stands on the floor in front of the children. Beginning at one end of the row, she pulls each child from the bench, letting her remain in whatever position she falls. Sometimes she can tell them how to pose, for instance, she will say 'Like an angel', and that child will fold her hands and look upward. Another might be 'cross school-teacher', and this child may pretend to be scolding someone. Each child remains perfectly still, posed in the attitude suggested, until all the children are on the floor. Then the leader selects the one she thinks has posed the best and that one takes the leader's place and the game goes on as before.

OUR COOK DOESN'T LIKE PEAS.

All the players except one sit in a row. This one sits in front of them and says to each one in turn: 'Our cook doesn't like P's; what can you give her instead?'

The first one may answer 'sugar' and that will suit her, but the next one might say 'potatoes', and that will not do, and he will have to pay a forfeit because the letter 'P' comes in that word.

There is a catch to this as everyone thinks that the vegetable 'peas' is meant instead of the letter. Even after everybody has discovered the trick it will be difficult to think of words, and if a player fails to answer before 5 is counted, a forfeit must be paid. 'My grandma doesn't like tea (T)' is played in the same way.

HOLD FAST, LET GO.

A simple game for small children is the following. Each child takes hold of a small sheet or tablecloth, the leader holding it with his left hand, while he pretends to write with his right hand.

The leader says: 'When I say "Hold fast," let go; and when I say "Let go," hold fast.' He calls out the commands one at a time and the rest do just the opposite of what he says. Whoever fails must pay a forfeit.

SIMON SAYS.

One child is selected to be Simon. The rest of the children sit around in a circle. Simon stands in the middle and gives all sorts of orders for the children to follow. Every order which begins with 'Simon says' must be obeyed, whether Simon performs it or not, but if Simon should give some order, such as 'thumbs down', whether he puts his thumbs down or not, it must not be obeyed by the others because it was not preceded by 'Simon says'.

All sorts of orders such as 'thumbs up', 'thumbs down', 'thumbs wiggle-waggle', 'thumbs pull left ear', etc., are given. The faster the orders are given, the more confusing it is. A forfeit must be paid by those who fail to obey the orders.

OLD SOLDIER.

One child, who represents the old soldier, goes around to each child in turn and begs for something, saying that he is poor, hungry, blind, etc., and asks what they will do for him.

In answering the old soldier no one must use the words, 'Yes', 'No', 'Black', or 'White'. As soon as a child is asked, he must answer immediately. If he does not, or says any of the forbidden words, he must pay a forfeit.

HIDE AND SEEK.

One child is chosen out. This one stands by a post or in a corner which is called 'base', and hides his eyes. The children decide among themselves how much he shall count while they are hiding. Suppose they choose 100, then he counts 5, 10, 15, 20, etc., until he reaches 100, and then he calls out:

Ready or not,
You shall be caught.

Each child having hidden in some place while he was counting, remains perfectly still while he is hunting for them. If he passes by some child without finding him, that one can run to the 'base' and say 'One, two, three, I'm in free!' As many children as can try to get in 'free', but if the one who is out tags any of them before they reach 'base', the first one tagged is the next to hide his eyes.

HANG–MAN.

Two children may derive a great deal of amusement from this simple pastime. At the top of a piece of paper write all the letters of the alphabet. Underneath, the child who has thought of a word or short sentence puts a dash down for every letter contained in the word thought of.

Suppose the words thought of were 'Gamebook', it would be written thus: - - - - - - - -

The other player asks if the word contains 'a', and the other puts it in its proper place, crossing the letter off of the alphabet above. The other guesses different letters at random, every right one being put in its place, while for every wrong one a line is drawn to help construct a gallows for the 'hang-man'. If there are many wrong guesses, the 'hang-man' may be completed and then the word is told to the other player. The players take turns in giving out and guessing the words.

The gallows is made thus for every wrong guess:

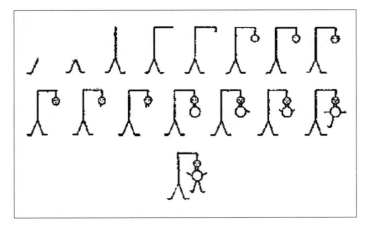

BIRD, BEAST, OR FISH.

A simple little game for amusing two children is the following. Write on the top of a slate or paper the words 'Bird, beast, and fish'.

One child thinks of the name of some animal and puts down the first and last letters of the word, marking dashes for the other letters. His companion thinks over all the names of animals he knows containing that number of letters, until finally he has guessed what it is or else has given up. If he guesses correctly it is his turn to give either a bird, beast, or fish.

PETER PIPER.

This is an amusing game for children. A blackboard is needed upon which the verse, 'Peter Piper', etc., is illustrated or written so that the words are mixed up and it will be difficult to point out. Some older person will be needed to superintend the game.

One child is given a pointer and as the others sing, to any familiar tune (Yankee Doodle, for instance):

  Peter Piper picked a peck of pickled peppers,
  Now if Peter Piper picked a peck of pickled peppers,
   Where is that peck of pickled peppers,
   Peter Piper picked?

She must point out each word or drawing as quickly as it is sung.

If a mistake is made in pointing, the child takes her place with the rest and another child is out. Each one is given a turn.

It is an achievement, if done successfully, and some suitable gift should be given as a prize.

LOOK OUT FOR THE BEAR!

Any number of children can play this game. One is chosen to be the 'bear', and he hides in some part of the room or garden, while the rest, with their backs turned, are standing at their goal.

As soon as the children have counted 50 or 100, they all scatter and hunt for the 'bear'. The child who finds him first calls out, 'Look out for the bear', and all the children run to their goal.

If the bear catches any while running for the goal, they become 'bears'. These 'bears' hide together and the game continues until all the children are 'bears'.

HOOP RACE.

All children love to roll hoops. For a little folks party, plan to have as many hoops as children, so each can have one.

Bind these around with tape or ribbon. The children contest one at a time. The child who succeeds in rolling his hoop around the room three times without having it turn over or stop, wins the prize.

If the room is very large once or twice around will be enough, so the children aren't tired out.

BUTTON FUN.

An amusement for small children is to gather together as many buttons of all shapes and sizes, plain and fancy, as can be obtained.

The largest button is the father, the next size is the mother, several children arranged according to size, and a tiny one for the baby.

Plain buttons are called servants, others animals and pets. The children arrange their families in pasteboard boxes, using pasteboard cards for chairs, carriages, etc. All children like to play 'house', and a whole afternoon can be whiled away making stores out of cards, to do shopping in, and boats for the button-children to play in. 'School' also can be played and the boys enjoy forming rows of soldiers and parading up and down.

STEPS.

One child is chosen out. This one stands by a post or door with his back to the other players. The rest of the children stand in a row at the other end of the room or porch, as the case may be.

The one by the door counts five, slowly or quickly, and then turns around. While he is counting and his back is turned, the others take as many steps forward as they can without being caught. If anyone is moving when the player turns around, they exchange places, and the game continues, the children advancing step by step toward the goal. When one has reached the goal and touched it, he can go back again and begin all over. The one who touches the goal the greatest number of times just by stepping, and has not been caught, wins the game.

HE CAN DO LITTLE.

All the players sit in a circle. One, knowing the catch, begins by saying: 'Ahem, he can do little who cannot do this.' While saying this, he taps a stick on the floor several times.

This stick passes from one to the other in turn, each one thinking that the stick must be tapped a certain number of times, but the catch is that just before saying 'He can do little who cannot do this', each one ought to clear his throat as the leader did at first. Allow the game to continue around the circle two or three times before explaining the catch. A forfeit is paid by each player who does not do it correctly.

WINK.

All the girls sit in a circle, and the boys stand outside, one boy behind each girl's chair. One chair is left vacant, but a boy stands behind it, and by winking at the girls one at a time, tries to get one for his empty chair.

As soon as a girl is winked at, she tries to leave her seat, and take the vacant one, but if the boy behind her touches her before she leaves the seat, she cannot go. Each boy has to keep his eye on the one who is winking and on the girl in his chair, for if he is not watching, she may escape before he has time to touch her, and then it is his turn to do the winking and get a girl for his chair.

If the winking is done quickly it adds to the interest of the game. No boy can keep hold of a girl all the time; he must only touch her when she starts to leave her place, and then if she is beyond arm's length, he cannot call her back.

DOUBLE TAG.

The children stand in pairs, one behind the other, in the form of a circle, all facing the centre.

Two of them are out, one who runs away, and the other who tries to catch him. The one who is running away may place himself in front of any couple for safety and he cannot be tagged, but the child at the end of the trio must run, and if he is caught before he can stand in front of another couple, he is the catcher and pursues the other child.

PUSS IN THE CORNER.

All the children except one stand in corners, or in any fixed stations if there are not enough corners to go around. The one who is out stands in the middle to represent 'Puss'. The players then beckon to each other one at a time saying, 'Here, puss, puss', and run and change places with the one who is called.

Puss tries to get one of the vacant places. If she succeeds, the child who is left out is 'Puss', until she manages to obtain a place.

I HAVE A BASKET.

One child begins by saying: 'I have a basket.' The one to his left says: 'What is in it?' The first one replies with the name of some article beginning with 'a', such as 'apples'.

No.2 says: 'I have a basket', and the next one to him says: 'What is in it?' No.2 replies: 'Apples and bananas', (or some other word beginning with 'b').

No.3 says: 'I have a basket.' No.4 asks the same question as before and No.3 responds with 'Apples, bananas, and cats', and so on, each in turn repeating what the others have said, and adding another article, which commences with the next letter of the alphabet. Whoever forgets what the other articles were must pay a forfeit. Thus it continues until the last one has named all the articles in order, and ended with 'z'.

STILL POND, NO MORE MOVING.

All the children form a circle, joining hands. One is blindfolded, given a cane, and stands in the middle of the circle.

The children march around her, going fast or slowly until she taps on the floor three times with the cane and says: 'Still pond, no more moving.' The children drop hands, and remain perfectly still, right where they are.

The one in the middle feels her way toward the children, holding the cane in front of her. The first child who is touched with the cane must take hold of it. The blindfolded one says, 'Grunt like a pig', and the one holding the cane must grunt, disguising her voice if possible. If the blindfolded one guesses who she is, they exchange places, and the game goes on as before, but if she fails, she has another turn and may tell the player to 'Bark like a dog' or 'Mew like a cat' until she guesses the right one.

RING ON A STRING.

Slip a ring on a long piece of string having the ends knotted together. The players stand in a circle and the string passes through their closed hands. Each makes the motions of passing something.

The ring circulates from one to another, while a player in the middle tries to find it. As soon as the ring is found, the person in whose hands it was takes his place, and the ring is passed as before.

HUNT THE SLIPPER.

All the children except one sit on the floor in a circle, with their knees raised. The one left out brings a slipper, and handing it to one child says:

> Cobbler, cobbler, mend my shoe,
> Get it done by quarter-past two.

He walks to the other side of the room and in a minute comes back and asks if the shoe is done. In the meantime the slipper is being passed from one to the other, under their knees.

The child who is asked if the slipper is done says she thinks her neighbour has it, the neighbour is asked and receiving the same answer the one hunting it goes from one to the other until the slipper is found. If it takes too long for him to find it, the slipper may be tossed across the circle, so it will be easy to follow it up.

WHAT IS MY THOUGHT LIKE?

All the children except one sit in a circle. This one thinks of something and, standing in the middle of the circle, asks each one in turn: 'What is my thought like?'

Each one names some object, and when all have been asked, the leader announces what her thought was and each in turn must prove the resemblance between his answer and the thought. Whoever fails must pay a forfeit.

Suppose the thought is a stove, and No.1 says: 'Like the sun'. No.2, 'Like silver', then the second time around No.1 can say: 'A stove is like the sun because they both give heat'; No.2 can say: 'A stove is like silver because they both shine when well polished', and so on.

ORANGES AND LEMONS.

The two tallest children, one named 'Orange', the other 'Lemon', join hands and form an arch for the other children to pass under. The children, holding on to each other's dresses, march in single file and sing:

'Oranges and lemons,' say the bells of St Clement's,
'Brickbats and tiles,' say the bells of St Giles,
'You owe me five farthing,' say the bells of St Martin's,
'When will you pay me?' say the bells of Old Bailey,
'When I grow rich,' say the bells of Shoreditch,
'When will that be?' say the bells of Stepney,
'I do not know,' says the great bell of Bow.
Here comes a candle to light you to bed,
And here comes a chopper to chop off your head.

When the last line is sung the child who is under their arms is caught and asked in a whisper if he will be an orange or lemon. He answers, and joins whichever side he chose, holding the other around the waist. The game continues until all are caught, and then there is a tug-of-war between the oranges and lemons.

RED–HOT POTATO.

The 'potato' in this game is a knotted handkerchief. One player is chosen for the centre, and the others sit around in a circle. The one in the centre throws the 'potato' to anyone in the circle. This one must throw it to another player and so on, tossing it, from one to another, and never allowing it to rest.

The player in the centre tries to catch it. If he succeeds, the one who last tossed it exchanges places with him, and the game goes on as before.

JUDGE AND JURY.

Arrange the children in two rows, facing each other. The judge sits at one end in the aisle. He asks one of the jury a question (anything he happens to think of). The one who is questioned must not answer, but the child sitting opposite him must reply for him, being careful not to use any of the following words in his answer: Yes, no, black, or white. Some answer must be given, whether it be sensible, or not.

Whoever fails to answer before the judge counts 10, or answers out of turn, or uses any of the forbidden words must either pay a forfeit or become the judge.

REUBEN AND RACHEL.

Blindfold one of the players. All the rest form a ring and dance around him until he points at someone. That one enters the ring and the blind-man calls out: 'Rachel'; she answers: 'Here, Reuben', and moves about in the circle so as to escape being caught by 'Reuben'.

Every time the blindman calls out 'Rachel', she must reply with 'Reuben' and thus it goes until finally 'Rachel' is caught. 'Reuben' must guess who she is, and if he guesses correctly, 'Rachel' is blindfolded and the game goes on as before. If not, the same child is 'Reuben' again.

FROG IN THE MIDDLE.

The children form a ring. One, the frog, is chosen out, and he stands in the middle of the circle.

The children, holding hands, dance around him, saying: 'Frog in the middle, jump in, jump out, take a stick and poke him out.' As the last line is sung, the frog takes one child by the hands and pulls him to the centre, exchanging places with him. The children continue dancing around and singing while the frogs jump thick and fast. The game continues until all have been frogs or are tired out.

HORSEMEN.

This is a rough-and-tumble game for the boys, and must be played either outside, or in a large bare room.

Sides are chosen, the big boys taking the small boys on their back, carrying them 'pick-a-back'. The one carrying the boy is called the horse, and the other the rider. The sides stand opposite each other and when a signal is given, they rush toward each other, the horses trying to knock down the opposing horses, and the riders trying to dismount each other.

The game continues until a single horse and rider remain, and the side to which they belong wins the game.

MY HOUSE, YOUR HOUSE.

Attach a string to the end of a small stick. At the end of the string make a loop that will slip very easily. On a table make a circle with chalk.

The leader, or fisherman, arranges the loop around the circle and holds the stick in his hand. Whenever he says 'My house', each player must put his first finger inside the circle, and leave it there. When 'Your house' is said, the fingers must be withdrawn.

The commands must be given very quickly, and the fisherman must be quick to jerk his rod, thus catching several fingers.

A forfeit should be paid by everyone who is caught, and the fisherman can exchange places if he wishes.

MALAGA GRAPES.

All the players sit in a circle and one who knows the trick takes a small cane in his right hand; then, taking it in his left hand, he passes it to his neighbour, saying: 'Malaga grapes are very good grapes; the best to be had in the market.' He tells his neighbour to do the same.

Thus the cane passes from one to the other, each one telling about the grapes; but if any should pass the stick with the right hand, a forfeit must be paid. The trick must not be told until it has gone around the circle once or twice.

PART II

Games for Adults

SPOON PICTURES.

It will be necessary for two of the players to know how to play the game. One is sent out of the room, and the other remains inside to take a picture of one of the guests. This is done by holding up a spoon or some polished surface to a player's face.

When the picture is taken, the one outside is called in, given the spoon, told to look at it, and guess whose picture it is. In a short time she has guessed correctly, to the amazement of the guests. She leaves the room again, while another picture is taken, is called in, and guesses that, and so on.

If any guest thinks he can do it, he may have a trial, but he may fail. Finally it is discovered that the one who remained inside and took the pictures sits in exactly the same position as the person whose picture was taken. If his feet were crossed and his hands folded, the leader will take that position. If another person is in that position, the one who guesses waits until one makes a change, and thus the name may be guessed.

BOOTS, WITHOUT SHOES.

All the players are sent out of the room. The leader remains inside and calls one player in. They both sit down together and the leader says: 'Say just what I say. Say boots, without shoes.' (With a short pause after boots.) The victim may repeat the whole sentence and the leader says, 'No, I want you to say boots, without shoes', and thus it may go on until the leader has given the simple statement in all sorts of tones and expressions, and finally, the player realises that when told to say 'Boots, without shoes', she must simply say 'Boots'.

Each player in turn is called in and put through the ordeal, affording much amusement for those already in the room, until all have guessed it and laughed over it.

PROVERBS.

Any number of persons may play this game. One is sent out of the room while the rest choose some proverb. Then he is called in and asks each player in turn a question. In the answer, no matter what the question is, one word of the proverb must be given.

Suppose the proverb 'Make hay while the sun shines' is taken, then player No.1 would have 'Make'; No.2, 'hay'; No.3, 'while'; No.4, 'the'; No.5, 'sun'; No.6, 'shines'; No.7, 'make'; etc., giving each player a word, often repeating the proverb several times.

The answers to the questions must be given quickly, and no special word emphasised. Often the one guessing will have to go around several times before he can discover any word which will reveal the proverb. The one whose answer gave the clue must leave the room next, and it becomes his turn to guess.

ANIMAL, VEGETABLE, MINERAL.

When the party is large, this game affords much amusement. One player is sent out of the room. While he is gone the players decide upon some object which he is to guess. He is then called in, and asks each one a question.

The answers to the questions must be either 'Yes' or 'No', and a forfeit must be paid if any other answer is given.

Suppose the object chosen is a piece of coal in the fireplace. The player will begin by finding out whether the object chosen is of the animal, vegetable, or mineral kingdom; thus the following questions may be asked: 'Is it a mineral?' 'Yes.' 'Is it hard?' 'Yes.' 'Is it very valuable?' 'No.' 'Is it bright and shiny?' 'Yes.' 'Is it gold?' 'No.' 'Silver?' 'No.' 'Is it in this room?' 'Yes.' 'Is it black?' 'Yes.' 'Is it a piece of coal?' 'Yes.'

The correct object being guessed, another player is sent out and the game continues.

WHAT TIME IS IT?

It requires two players who understand this game, a leader and his accomplice. The accomplice leaves the room, while the leader and the rest remain inside. The leader asks the players what hour they will choose for the accomplice to guess. One will say: '4 o'clock'. The assistant is called in and he questions the leader, saying: 'Well, what time is it?' The leader answers thus: 'Don't you know?'; next, 'Doubtless, dancing time.' The assistant immediately answers '4 o'clock', to the amazement of the company.

The key is that each hour, from 1 to 12 o'clock has been named according to the letters of the alphabet in rotation, from A to K. The leader, in answering, must be very careful to begin each answer with the letter indicating the chosen hour; thus in the above the assistant noticed that each answer began with 'd', and 'd' being the fourth letter, 4 o'clock was the time chosen. Only the exact hours must be chosen. As the different players think they understand the game, they may take the assistant's place, and many ludicrous mistakes will be the result until the game has been explained to all.

IT.

One of the players who does not know the game is sent out of the room. While he is gone, the others are supposed to be thinking of some person whom he is to guess when he comes in, but it is arranged that each one describes his right-hand neighbour when asked any questions. It is more amusing if the circle is composed of boys and girls alternating.

The player is called in, having been told beforehand that he is to guess what person the company thought of and that that person is 'It'.

He begins by asking 'Is it in this room?' 'Yes.' 'Is it a boy?' 'Yes.' 'Is his hair long or short?' 'Very long', and so on, until the information he has obtained may be the following: 'A boy, very long hair, pink waist, blue eyes, has a beard, very stout, about 6 feet tall, about 8 years old.' The player, astonished at such information, may keep up guessing, until, by closely questioning each one, he guesses correctly. If he cannot guess, it is explained to him who 'It' is.

HOW, WHEN, WHERE.

One of the players leaves the room while the others select some word with two or three meanings, which is to be guessed. Suppose the word 'trunk' is thought of. When the player is summoned in he asks each one in turn 'How do you like it?' The answers may be 'full of clothes', 'when the outside is brown', (meaning a tree trunk), 'shut up in a cage', (referring to an elephant's trunk).

The next time around the question is 'When do you like it?' and the answers may be, 'When I'm going away', 'When I'm in the country', 'When I visit the zoo.'

The last question is 'Where do you like it?' and the answers may be 'In my room', 'In the woods', 'On the animal it belongs to.' The questioner must try to guess the word from the various answers. If he succeeds, the person whose answer revealed the word must leave the room, but if he fails, he has to guess again.

BUZ.

All the players sit in a circle and begin to count in turn, but whenever seven, or any multiple of seven comes, 'Buz' is said in its place. If anyone forgets he may be put out and the game commenced over again, but it is more fun if the players go right on with the counting, as many will fall off when the count is up in the hundreds. The game may be continued as long as is desired.

Suppose the players have counted up to twenty, the next one would say 'Buz', as twenty-one is a multiple of seven; the next, 'twenty-two', the next 'twenty-three', and so on. The one having 'twenty-seven' would say 'Buz', as it contains seven. When seventy is reached, the numbers are said, 'Buz one', 'Buz two', etc.; 'double Buz', for seventy-seven, and so on.

'Siz' may be substituted for six and its multiples, and 'Fiz' for five, just for variety.

JENKINS UP!

Divide the company into two sides. One division sits around the table on one side, the other on the opposite side. The members of division 'A' put their hands under the table and a small coin is passed from one to the other.

When division 'B' thinks they have had enough time, the players call out, 'Jenkins up!' and the players of 'A' hold up their closed hands, and when 'Jenkins down!' is called, they must place their hands, palm down, on the table. The players of 'B' must guess under which palm the coin is. Each player has one guess, those on the opposite side raising their hands when requested to do so.

If 'B' guesses correctly, the coin is passed over to them and 'A' must guess who has it, but if not, 'A' keeps the coin, and 'B' has another trial for guessing.

Tally may be kept, 1 being counted for every correct guess, and a certain number, such as 50, may be the limit. The side gaining 50 points first is victorious.

PREFIXES.

One of the players is sent out of the room. The others then decide upon some word which he is to guess when he returns. He is told what the prefix of the word is, and must guess, by asking questions, what the rest of the word is. The players answer his questions by their manner or actions.

Suppose the word chosen is 'encouraged', the answers may be given in a cheerful way.

The player who is guessing may think of any number of words with the prefix 'en', but he must continue asking questions until the right word has been guessed.

The player who has revealed the word by his or her actions, takes the other's place and leaves the room while the rest are deciding upon some word for him to guess. The game continues as before.

MY FATHER HAD A ROOSTER.

All the players sit in a circle, the leader begins by saying, 'My father had a rooster!' The player to his left says: 'A what?' The leader answers: 'A rooster!' Each player repeats this in turn to his left-hand neighbour who asks the question, until it is the leader's turn again.

He then repeats the first part and asks the player next to him, 'Could he crow?' The player answers, 'Crow he could.' This is repeated by each player with the previous questions. The next time the leader says 'How could he crow?' The player on the left answers 'Cock-a-doodle-doo!' This goes around the circle again and when the last one has taken part, all together say 'Cock-a-doodle-doo', as a finish.

No one is supposed to laugh during the whole game, whoever does, may either pay a forfeit or is out of the game. It is best to have a person who knows the game sit next to the leader, so they can start the game correctly. The complete statements are these,

'My father had a rooster!'
'A what?'
'A rooster!'
'Could he crow?'
'Crow he could!'
'How could he crow?'
'Cock-a-doodle-doo!'

CROSS QUESTIONS AND CROOKED ANSWERS.

All sit in a circle for this game. The first one begins by whispering some question to his left hand neighbour, such as 'Do you like apples?' The second player must remember the question asked of him, and he answers No. 1 by saying, 'Yes, the nice, red, juicy kind.' This answer belongs to No. 1 and he must remember it. No. 2 asks No. 3 a question, being careful to remember his answer, as it belongs to him. Suppose he asks, 'Are you fond of books?' and the answer is 'Yes, I read every one that comes out.' Thus No. 2 has a question and answer that belong to him.

Every one in turn asks a question and gives an answer, remembering the question he was asked and the answer his neighbour gave him, which belong to him. When all have had a turn, No. 2 begins by saying aloud: 'I was asked: "Do you like cats?" and the answer was "Yes, the nice, red juicy kind";' No. 2 says: 'I was asked, "Do you like apples?" and the answer was, "Yes, I read every one that comes out,"' and so on.

MAGIC WRITING.

An assistant is necessary for this game. One gives a little talk about sign-language and says that he can read any sign made with a stick on the floor, and will leave the room while the others decide upon some word for him to guess.

Beforehand, it has been agreed upon between the leader and his assistant that one tap of the stick on the floor will represent 'a'; two taps, 'e'; three taps, 'i'; four taps, 'o'; five taps, 'u'. Thus all the vowels are indicated by taps, and the consonants, by having the first word of the sentence which the leader gives begin with the chosen letter. The letters of the chosen word must be given in order.

The leader, who remains inside, knows the chosen word, and when the assistant is called in, he makes many signs with the stick, tapping in the proper places.

Suppose the word chosen is 'Games'. When the assistant is called in, the leader begins by making many scrolls, etc., on the floor, then says: 'Great fun, isn't it?' (initial letter 'g'), then one tap, 'a'; 'Many don't know what I'm writing', (initial letter 'm'); 2 taps, 'e'; 'Sometimes it is hard to read', (initial letter 's'). Then a few more marks, so as not to end too abruptly, and the assistant says 'Games', to the astonishment of the company.

This is continued until some have guessed, or until the trick has been explained.

FAMOUS NUMBERS.

Provide the players with pencil and paper. Each one writes a number on his slip. The papers are collected, mixed up, and each player draws one. Each in turn must name something or someone suggested by that number. The one who is unable to name anything must pay a forfeit.

Suppose No. 1 has 4, he will say: 'My number is 12; there are 12 months in a year.' No. 2, 'My number is 14; 14 February is Valentine's Day.' No. 3, 'My number is 60; there are 60 minutes in an hour.'

MAGIC ANSWERS.

One is sent from the room and the others decide upon some object which is to be guessed when the player enters.

The player outside has an accomplice in with the others who asks the question when he returns. It was arranged between them that the object chosen should be named after some four-legged thing.

Suppose a book is chosen by the players. When summoned in, the accomplice asks: 'Is it anyone in this room?' 'No.' 'Is it a handkerchief?' 'No.' 'Is it a picture?' 'No.' 'Is it a dog?' 'No.' 'Is it this book?' 'Yes.'

Another arrangement is to have the correct object mentioned after something which is black, such as shoes, ink, etc.

MODELLING.

Provide each player with a card and a toothpick, also a piece of gum, or paraffin if preferred.

The hostess announces that when she says 'Ready', the gum is to be chewed until she tells them to stop, and then each one is to take the gum, place it upon the card, and with the aid of the toothpick, model either an animal or a flower, keeping his selection a secret, as each one can choose what he wishes to model. The hostess keeps an eye on the time and when time is up, (any length she chooses) all the cards are collected and placed on a table for exhibition.

There is a curious mixture of cows, cats, dogs, sunflowers, pansies, violets, etc. Vote is taken upon the best model and a prize is awarded the victor.

SCISSORS CROSSED OR UNCROSSED.

A simple catch game is as follows. It is best if two of the company know how to play it. One of the two is the leader and the other helps her out.

The leader hands a closed pair of scissors to her accomplice, who takes it and says: 'I received these scissors uncrossed and I give them crossed.' (Opening the scissors as she speaks.) She passes them to the player on her right who should say: 'I receive these scissors crossed and I give them crossed.' (If they are left open; if closed, they are uncrossed.) Those who do not know the game receive the scissors and pass them and say what they think they ought. It may be just what the player before said, but the condition of the scissors may not be the same, and, therefore, it is not right.

Thus each one has a turn, and the game continues until some bright player notices that the scissors are called crossed when they are open and uncrossed when they are closed, and that the player who knows the game crossed her feet if the scissors were crossed, and if not, her feet were uncrossed, or resting on the floor as usual.

Thus the object of the game is to change the words and the position of the feet in accordance with the position of the scissors.

CAPPING VERSES.

To while away the time before dinner, or while sitting in the twilight, this is a simple amusement for those who love poetry.

One begins by giving a line or verse of poetry. The next one continues, but his verse must commence with the last letter of the previous verse, and so on, each one capping the other's verse.

Suppose No.1 quotes:

> Full many a flower is born to blush unseen
> And waste its sweetness on the desert air.

No.2 continues quoting:

> Romeo! wherefore art thou Romeo?

No.3:

> O speak again, bright angel.

No.4:

> Like summer tempest came her tears,
> 'Sweet, my child, I live for thee.'

and so on until the guests tire of it.

RABBIT.

The leader, who knows the game, asks each one in turn: 'Do you know how to play rabbit?' When all have answered, he says: 'Do just what I do, and I will show you how.'

1st. All stand in a row.

2nd. All kneel down on one knee.

3rd. All place the first finger of the right hand on the floor.

When all the players are in this position, just as they are losing their balance, the leader, who is at the head of the line, pushes against the player next to him, thus knocking over the whole row. As they fall amid laughter, he calmly announces that that is the way to play rabbit.

GHOST.

Turn down the lights. All the players sit in a circle. The leader has a button which she gives to some player, as in 'Button, button, who has the button?' The one who guesses who has the button takes the leader's place while the leader becomes a ghost and remains outside the circle. She can talk to the players in the circle, but no one except the one in the middle can answer her. Anyone who does, becomes a ghost with the leader.

Every effort is made on the part of the ghosts to induce the players to answer. The button keeps going around the inside circle, the one depositing the button becoming a ghost when a correct answer is given and the other one taking his place.

The game continues until all are ghosts. If there was one who was not enticed, that one wins the game.

WHAT AM I?

One of the players is sent out of the room. The rest decide upon the name of some animal which he is to guess.

When he returns the players question him in turn, imitating the habits of the animal chosen and asking questions as if he were that animal.

For instance, the animal chosen is tiger. The questions may be, 'Do you scratch?' 'Are your claws sharp?' 'Do you howl at night?' etc. The player thinking they have named him a cat answers, 'Yes', and says, 'Am I a cat?' When answered in the negative, the players still question him until he finally guesses tiger. The player whose question betrayed the name of the chosen animal then takes his place and the game continues as before.

NEEDLE THREADING.

Procure several large jars. Stand these on their sides. Only men can contest for this, as ladies are supposed to be expert needle-threaders.

Four or five men contest at a time. Each sits on a jar with his feet crossed in front. The leader hands each a needle and thread. Allow five minutes for the contest.

The jars, being on their sides, will roll around, and as the contestants have their feet crossed, it is a difficult task to remain still long enough to thread the needle. Those who succeed deserve some sort of prize.

CONFUSIONS.

The players are provided with pencil and paper. Each player selects the name of some animal, fish, or bird, and mixes the letters so as to spell other words. For instance, if one chooses elephant, the words might be 'pent heal'; if monkey, 'o my ken', while mackerel may be 'mere lack'.

Allow five minutes for making the 'confusion', no letter can be used twice, and words must be formed. Then the hostess rings the bell and each player in turn reads his 'confusion' to the rest who guess what his chosen word is. Each puzzle is carefully timed. The one whose puzzle takes longest to guess is the winner, therefore, each person must mix the letters as much as possible.

Sides may be chosen if preferred, the players taking turn alternately, the side which has taken the least time to guess the puzzles is the victorious side.

VERBAL AUTHORS.

The players sit in a circle. One is chosen as judge and he keeps tally. Each player in turn, rises, and names some well-known book. The first one to call out the name of the author scores a point. The game continues until the interest ceases or the store of literary knowledge is exhausted. The player having the most points is the winner.

This game may be played in another way. Instead of calling out the author as the book is named, provide each guest with pencil and paper and announce that as a book is named, each player must write down the author and the name of some character in that book.

Examples:

The Taming of the Shrew
Wm. Shakespeare – Petruchio.

Nicholas Nickleby
Chas. Dickens – Mr Squeers.

Ivanhoe
Sir Walter Scott – Rebecca.

PIN DOLL BABIES.

Any number may play this game. If there are men and women it is
more amusing.

Divide the company into groups of five or six. Each group sits around
a table upon which are pins, needles and thread, scissors, for each player
but no thimbles, and strips of tissue paper, coloured and white.

The hostess hands each guest a large wooden clothes-pin which is to
be dressed as a doll, using the tissue paper for dresses and hats.

All begin to work at a given signal and the hostess allows a certain
length of time for the dressmaking. There is much merriment, as it is
nearly as awkward for the ladies to sew without a thimble as it is for
the men to use a needle.

When the time is up, these doll babies are arranged in line for inspection. Two judges are appointed to decide upon the best and the worst.
Prizes are awarded.

BUILDING SENTENCES.

The hostess begins by saying one word and announces that each word
of the sentence must begin with the initial letter of the given word.
The player to her right gives the second word, the next player, the third,
and so on, until the sentence is complete only when it reaches the
hostess.

Each player must be careful not to give a word which, with the others,
completes the sentence, as the hostess is the only one who is supposed to
finish it – but sometimes it seems as though all the words of that letter

have been taken; if this is the case, the player who finished the sentence must pay a forfeit or drop out of the game.

Suppose there are nine players and number one says 'An', number two 'Angry', number three 'Ape', number four 'Ate', number five 'Apples'; thus number five is out or pays a forfeit as the sentence is completed and there are still four more to play. Thus the sentence might have been 'An angry ape ate attractive, audacious, ancient April apples.'

This sentence is absurd, but the more ridiculous, the greater the fun.

For the second turn the player to the right of the hostess begins, using a word beginning with another letter and so on, until each player has started a sentence.

GEOGRAPHY.

Select two leaders from the company. Each leader chooses players for his side. The sides stand opposite each other. One leader begins by giving the name of some river, mountain, lake, city or town, county or country, located in any part of the world, that begins with the letter A, the other leader answers back with another geographical name commencing with A. The two leaders continue with the letter A until they can think of no more names, then, they commence with B, and so on, until every letter of the alphabet has been used.

The players on the opposite sides simply help their leader with the names, as soon as one thinks of a name it is passed up to the leader to help him. No place can be named twice. The side that stands up the longest wins.

Another way to play this game is as follows. Having chosen the sides as before, one leader begins by naming any place, lake, river, etc., commencing with any letter; the leader on the other side then follows with a name commencing with the last letter of the previous name; then the player next to the leader on the opposite side follows with a name commencing with the last letter of that name and so on, each player has a turn as it goes from side to side. Suppose the leader names London, the next New York, and so on. Thirty seconds is allowed to think of a name, if he fails in that, he must drop out. Anyone may be challenged to locate the place which he has named. The side which has kept up the longest, is the champion.

WHAT WOULD YOU DO IF — ?

Predicaments of the worst kind are thought of and written on pieces of paper. These are handed among the guests, who write out an answer, telling the best way out of the difficulty. Each question begins with 'What would you do if — ?'

When all have written their answers, the papers are collected in a basket, mixed up, and each one draws one out. The answers are then read aloud.

Examples: 'What would you do if you fell into a tar barrel?' 'I would be too stuck up to do anything.'

'What would you do if you should meet a footpad?' 'I would say, "Please, sir, go away."'

WATCH TRICK.

It will require two people who know this game to be in the secret. One of them leaves the room while his confederate remains inside with the others. He hides an article which the rest of the players have selected, in an adjoining room which is totally dark, placing a watch with a moderately loud tick, either on, or as near to the hidden object as he can. The rest of the players must not know anything about the watch, as they are kept guessing how the player who is out, succeeds in finding the hidden article in the dark room.

When everything is ready, the one outside is called in, led into the dark room, and hunts for the object. The rest must remain very quiet, as it breaks the 'charm', so the leader says. Guided by the ticking of the watch, and knowing that it is there, he soon discovers the hidden object to the surprise of the others.

He and his confederate may take turns going out and after a while, if the company are very quiet, one of them might hear the watch ticking and the trick is disclosed.

FIND YOUR BETTER–HALF.

Select a number of pictures of men and women from fashion papers, advertising books, etc. If possible, try to procure them in pairs, that is, a man and woman contained in the same picture, or two having the same expression. Number the pictures in pairs, thus there will be two of No.1, of No.2, No.3, etc.

Give the young ladies the pictures of the men and the young men those of the ladies. Each one then hunts for his partner or 'better-half', comparing the pictures and number.

The more mixed the pictures were when given out, the longer it will take to find partners.

WORDS.

The players form a line as in a spelling match. Sides may be chosen if preferred. The first one begins by giving the first letter of a word, 'A' for instance, thinking of the word 'animal'. The next player, thinking of 'animate', says, 'n'. The next, thinking of 'antidote', says 't', but this with the other letters spells 'ant', so he must go to the foot of the line.

The object of the game is to keep from adding a letter which finishes the word. Often one will give a letter, when thinking of another word, which will complete a word. If he does not notice his mistake, the others call out 'foot'.

LETTERS.

Empty the contents of a box of 'anagrams' on a table so all the letters are in a pile face downward. The players sit around the table.

The leader begins by turning up one of the letters and says, 'Bird'. The players all see the letter, and the first one who responds with the name of a bird commencing with that letter is given the card, and then it is his turn to turn up a card, calling out 'Bird', 'Animal', 'Fish', or 'Famous Man', or anything he wishes. Suppose the first letter was 'E', and a player answered it with 'Eagle'; the next letter was 'G', and 'Famous Man' was called out, someone would say 'Grant'.

The one who has answered the most, thus obtaining the greatest number of cards, is the winner.

SEEING AND REMEMBERING.

Fill a table with all sorts of things, books, gloves, dolls, pins, scissors, food, some large, striking picture, another very small object. Keep the table covered until ready for use.

Then remove the cover and let all the guests march around it three times, touching nothing on it, simply looking. The cover is replaced and each one is given a pencil and paper on which he writes down as many things as he can remember were on the table.

The one who has the largest list of correct names receives a prize. The objects may be auctioned off afterwards.

LIVE TIT–TAT–TO.

On a sheet mark a regular tit-tat-to diagram in black point. Stretch the sheet so it will be smooth on the floor. Divide the company into sides, a captain being appointed for each side. Call one side the crosses and the other side the zeros.

When a signal is given, the captain of one side takes his position in any one of the squares of the diagram. The captain of the other side follows, taking his position, then a player of the first side takes his position endeavouring to be in a row with the first move, so the next player on his side will form the third cross or zero, as the case may be, in the row, either straight or diagonally, and win the game for that side.

The winning side then changes to zeros if they were crosses or vice versa. Let each player have a turn, as there are only nine squares, and as the game may be won before they are all filled, some may not have a chance to play. It is best, when playing a new game, to let those who did not play before have first play.

BITS OF ADVICE.

Each person is given a slip of paper and pencil. The leader then tells the players to write a bit of advice, original if possible, on the paper, fold it, and drop it into a basket as it passes by.

The papers are all mixed up and the basket is passed again, each player taking one, but not unfolding it until he is told to.

Before opening the papers each one must say whether the advice is good or bad, necessary or unnecessary, and whether he intends to follow it. When the paper is unfolded it may be the opposite of what he has said.

PICTURES.

Provide the players with pencil and paper. All sit in a circle. The leader announces that pictures are to be drawn in this manner. First, draw a head (either animal or human), fold the paper, pass it to the right.

Second – Draw a neck, shoulders, and arms.

Third – Complete the body (the former player having left two lines below the fold of the paper).

Fourth – The skirt, trousers or legs, as the case may be.

Fifth – The feet, and if you wish to add to the fun, the last one writes a name either of someone present or some noted person.

The papers are folded and passed after each drawing and the last time, they are all opened and passed around to be inspected and laughed over.

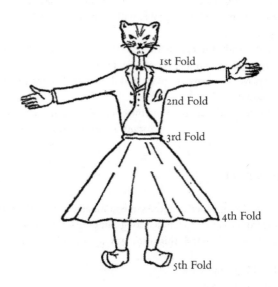

HOUSEHOLD GOSSIP.

One of the guests is sent out of the room. The hostess asks the remaining players to say something about him. As each one in turn gives his statement, she writes it down with the person's name on a piece of paper which she keeps.

The player is then summoned in and she reads the statements about him one at a time and he must try to guess who said it. As soon as he guesses one correctly, the one who said it must go out of the room and the game goes on as before.

Examples –

You have the family eyes.

Your chin is too small.

The left sleeve of your coat has a spot on it; and so on.

TABLE FOOTBALL.

The 'football' for this game is an eggshell which has had the egg blown out of it. The players sit around the table with their captains, who have been previously chosen at each end. There need not be just eleven on each side as in a regular game, but any number. Each captain chooses his side.

Boundaries are marked on the table with chalk or tape, the two ends being the goals.

When all are ready, the eggshell is placed in the middle of the table, a signal is given, and the members of each team blow the shell towards his goal. No player can leave his place, and the 'football' must be moved entirely by blowing.

Regular football rules are used and the count is the same as in football. It will add to the interest if the two teams stand for rival colleges.

MUSICAL MEDLEY.

Number eight slips of paper with the same number. On each slip write a part, or a line from a verse of a familiar song. Suppose set No. 1 was a verse of 'Land of Hope and Glory', this is the way it would be written.

1. Land of Hope and Glory,
1. Mother of the Free,

1. How shall we extol thee,
1. Who are born of thee?
1. Wider still and wider
1. Shall thy bounds be set;
1. God who make thee mighty,
1. Make thee mightier yet.

Prepare as many slips in groups of eight as there are guests. Give each one a slip at random and tell each to find the rest of his set.

When the players of one group have found each other, they stand together in one corner of the room and practise their song. Each group does this until all the groups are formed, and then, commencing with No. 1, each group in turn sings its song aloud for the benefit of the audience.

ANOTHER MUSICAL MEDLEY.

Provide each player with pencil and paper. Before playing this game it must be arranged with someone who plays the piano well to have a list of popular songs ready, which she must play one right after the other.

When the leader gives a signal, the pianist strikes up a tune and continues playing from a part of one song into another until she has reached the end of her list.

The others write down on their papers the names of the songs as fast as they are played, and when the pianist stops, the correct list is read by her, and the rest check off their lists. Prizes may be awarded. It is a strange fact, that after such a medley, there will be very few, if any, who have correct lists.

PASSING CLOTHESPINS.

Sides are chosen among the players. Each side then takes its position, forming a row on the floor, the leader at the end. The sides face each other, but quite a space is left between them.

At the head of each line is placed a basket containing twelve clothespins. Each player is instructed to hold his neighbour's right wrist with his left hand, thus leaving one hand (the right one), free.

The leaders begin by passing the clothespins, one at a time, down the line, each player being careful not to drop one. When one reaches the end of the line, the last player places it on the floor beside him until all twelve have been passed, then he passes them, the same as before, up the line to the leader.

The side which succeeds in passing all its clothespins back to its leader first is the victorious side. It is best to have a trial game first, so that the players may become used to passing with one hand, thus being able to do it rapidly for the regular game.

If a clothespin is dropped, the player who dropped it must pick it up and pass it on. The rest must wait until it is passed before passing any of the others.

PANTOMIME.

Give each guest a slip of paper, folded, containing words which can be acted in pantomime. Each one must keep his a secret, as the rest of the company guess what he is acting out.

The players sit in a circle, and the one acting in pantomime his words, stands in the middle where all can see him.

Suppose one had 'Dog' on his slip, he would pretend to pet him, call him, and make him perform. Another might have 'Blackberries' and make all the imaginary motions of picking and eating them, and being caught on the bushes. If one has 'Strawberry shortcake', she can go through the process of making the imaginary cake, and hulling the berries for it.

As soon as it is guessed what the player's word is, the rest call it out.

BIRDS FLY.

The players sit in a circle, one person who is quick and witty is chosen as leader. He stands in the centre of the circle.

Whenever he mentions any animal that flies all the players make a flying motion with their hands, but if he names something that doesn't fly, he alone makes the motions; if any player makes the motion when he ought to be still he is out of the game. Suppose the leader begins by saying 'Parrots fly', all must move their hands up and down whether the leader does or not, but if he says next time 'Horses fly', all must remain still.

It is a good plan to call the names quickly, inserting many that don't fly, when the players are excited, so they will be confused and many will be out.

TRIPS AROUND THE WORLD.

There are several ways of playing this game, here are two. Provide each guest with a little paper book to represent a guide book and a pencil.

Articles of all kinds have been scattered around the room to represent different countries, counties, or cities. A little package of tea suggests China; a paper fan, Japan; a wooden shoe, Holland; a stein, Germany; and so on. Allow a certain length of time for the guesses, then collect the little books, and the player who has guessed the greatest number correctly receives a prize.

Another way. The players sit in a circle, No. 1 names some place beginning with the letter A, and asks No.2 what he shall do there. No.2 answers in words beginning with A, and he, in turn names a city commencing with B, and asks No.3 the question. Thus each player must answer the question of his neighbour, and name another place.

For example:

'I am going to America, what shall I do there?'

'Admire Astrakhan Apples. I am bound for Boston, what shall I do there?'

'Bake beans and brown bread. My journey takes me to Chicago, what shall I do there?'

'Catch cold', etc., etc.

JACK'S ALIVE.

A piece of kindling wood is held in the fire until it is well lighted. It is then passed from one player to the other, each one saying in turn, 'Jack's alive.' The instant the stick ceases to burn 'Jack' is 'dead' and the one who is then holding it has to pay a forfeit.

It is passed very quickly from one to the other, as each player wishes to get rid of it before the spark goes out.

For a forfeit, the man who was holding it will have to undergo the process of having a black moustache made with the charred end of the stick.

GOING A–FISHING.

Cut a number of small fishes about two inches long out of cardboard. Each fish counts 5, but two, which may be a little larger, are numbered 10. A loop is made with thread on the back of each fish.

Rods (sticks about a foot long with string, at the end of which is a bent pin, fastened to each) are provided for the players.

The fishes are placed on the floor or table and, at the word 'Ready' from the leader, all the players go a-fishing. Each tries his best to hold his rod steady enough to slip the bent pin through the loop of thread. As soon as a fish is caught all must stop until the signal to begin again is given.

Everyone tries to catch the fishes marked 10, but sometimes it is wiser to catch as many ordinary ones as a person can, thus making more points. The player scoring most points is victor.

CONSEQUENCES.

Provide each player with pencil and paper. The first thing to write on the paper is an adjective which applies to a man. The paper is then folded over and passed to the right. This time each one writes the name of a man (either present or absent), folds the paper so the next one can't see what is written, and passes it on to the right. This is done each time and the order of names is as follows after the first two, then an adjective which applies to a lady, then a lady's name; next, where they met; what he said; then, what she said; the consequence; and last of all, what the world said.

After all have finished writing 'what the world said', the papers are passed to the right, opened, and read aloud.

Thus:

Handsome
Mr—
(met) Pretty
Miss—
(at) The Fair
(he said) Have you heard the news?
(she said) I intend to go home.
(the consequence was) They never spoke again.
(the world said) 'As you like it.'

PERSONAL CONUNDRUMS.

The guests are requested to think up some conundrums about some person in the present company.

Each one in turn gives his conundrum and the player to his left must answer it if he can; if he fails, anyone present may help him out.

The conundrums may be written if preferred, mixed up in a hat or basket and each player takes one to answer.

Some of them may prove very funny. For the best conundrum and best answer given, a prize may be awarded.

Examples –

Why is Mr— like Nelson's Column?
Because he is so very tall.

Why is Miss— like sugar?
Because she is easily melted, that is, overcome.

HUNTING THE WHISTLE.

The players who know how to play this game stay in one room, while the others go into the hall, or another room. Those knowing the trick sit down in chairs which have been arranged in two rows, with an aisle between.

The leader calls one in from the other room and explains to him that there is a whistle in the room, and as he hears it blown he must find it. He can make a long speech about the whistle so as to interest the player, because someone is then pinning the whistle, (which is on the end of a string) to the player's coat.

Both the leader and player stand at one end of the room, between the two rows of chairs. When the leader says 'Go', the player starts on his hunt. The rest of the players pretend they have the whistle, and blow it whenever it chances to pass their way. Thus the player is kept going from side to side until finally someone happens to pull the string and he feels it and discovers the whistle on his own coat. He then takes his place with the rest in the row and another one is called in and goes through the same hunt. Thus it continues until all the players know the game.

THE FIVE SENSES.

All the players sit in a circle. No.1 begins by naming something he has seen, being careful what his last word is, as it must furnish him with a rhyme for the rest of the game. Each player in turn tells what he has seen, then No.1 repeats his first statement and adds what he heard; the next time, what he tasted; then what he smelt; and lastly, what he felt. For example, No.1 says, 'I saw a ring of solid gold.' No.2 says, 'I saw a boy fall off the car.'

The second time round No.1 says,

> I saw a ring of solid gold.
> I heard a story twice told.

No.2 says,

> I saw a boy fall off the car.
> I heard the war news from afar.

and so on, after going around five times, No.1's complete rhyme would be,

> I saw a ring of solid gold.
> I heard a story twice told.
> I tasted cheese that was too old.
> I smelt hay that soon would mould.
> I felt for something I couldn't hold.

Do not have the verses written as there is more fun in trying to remember one's rhyme.

WIGGLES.

Provide each guest with pencil and paper. Papers four inches square will be large enough. Each player draws a line about an inch and a half long with one or more quirks in it, in the upper left hand corner of the paper.

The papers are then passed to the player to the right who must draw some picture out of the 'wiggle' in the corner. The paper may be turned in any position. Allow five minutes for the drawings.

At the end of this time, each one writes his name on the paper and hands it to the hostess. A committee is appointed to decide upon the best 'wiggle-picture' and a prize is awarded to the artist. Examples –

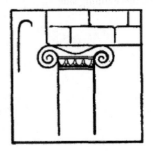 

The heaviest line is the wiggle.

TELEGRAM.

Provide the players with pencil and paper. Each one then writes on his piece of paper ten letters of the alphabet in any order, using no letter twice. The papers are then passed to the right and each one is requested to write a telegram, using the ten letters for the beginning of the ten words, just in the order given. The papers are then passed again and the telegrams are read aloud. Some will be very amusing.

Examples –

A. E. F. J. K. L. N. O. P. T. Am ever frightfully jealous. Keep lookout now on Pa's tricks.

C. B. D. W. G. H. S. I. M. Y. Come back. Down with Grandma. How shall I meet you?

SPELLING MATCH.

Choose leaders and divide the company into sides. The sides stand opposite each other as in the old-fashioned spelling match.

The leader, who may be the hostess, has a spelling book from which she selects the words which the players must spell backwards. Words of one or two syllables may be chosen, and if, when spelt backwards, they spell other words, so much the better.

The players take turns, one on one side, and one on the other, and so on, until all have spelled. If any fail to spell the word backwards, or do not pronounce it afterward, if it can be pronounced, they must drop out. The side which stands up the longest is the winning side.

Some words are:

Star	Now	Pan	Dew
Mat	Eve	Bard	Tub
Stop	Eel	Tops	Ton
Ten	On	Den	Nun

POOR PUSSY.

All the players sit in a circle, one being chosen out. This one kneels before each player in turn and says, in pitiful tones: 'Meow!' Each player, when addressed by 'Pussy', must say, without smiling: 'Poor Pussy.'

'Pussy' addresses each player three times, trying her best to make the players laugh. If the one she is kneeling before does laugh, they exchange places, but if not, 'Pussy' moves on to the next one.

GUESSES.

Each player receives a slip of paper and pencil. The leader begins by saying: 'Guess how high the door is'; 'Guess how thick that book is'; 'Guess how tall Mr Blank is'; 'How far does this chair stand from the floor?'

He allows a few seconds after each question for the players to write their answers. After twenty or more guesses have been asked, the papers are passed to the right-hand neighbour for correction.

The leader then measures each article, person, or thing, with a tape measure, and the guesses on the lists are checked off. The person who has a correct list deserves something for a reward.

NUT RACE.

Choose two captains from the company, who select sides until all the guests are on one side or the other.

Place a pile of mixed nuts on the floor and an empty bowl about three feet from it, at one end of the room and at the other end another pile and bowl.

The captains and their sides stand by their respective pile of nuts. When the signal is given each captain takes as many nuts on the back of his left hand from the pile as he can gather without the aid of his right hand and carries them to the empty bowl at the opposite side of the room. The players follow the captain in turn continuing until the pile is gone and the bowl is full.

The side which succeeds in filling its bowl first is victorious.

TORN FLOWERS.

Prepare a table full of different coloured tissue paper, bottles of mucilage and white cards, one for each guest.

The players sit around the table, the hostess gives each a card and announces that each one is to make a flower out of the tissue paper, but as there are no scissors each one must tear his paper and every one knows how hard it is to tear tissue paper. Each one keeps the name of his flower a secret. As they are made they are pasted on the cards. Each card is numbered and when all are done 'tearing', the cards are collected and placed on a table for exhibition.

The player guessing the greatest number of flowers correctly receives a prize. The game may be varied, as either animals or vegetables could be torn.

SPEARING PEANUTS.

Fill a cup with peanuts, two of which are blackened with ink on one end.

The guests play one at a time. No. 1 sits down by a table, empties the cup of peanuts in a pile on it and is given a hatpin with which she spears the peanuts one at a time without disturbing the pile, and places them back in the cup. A few minutes is allowed each player; when the time is up, the peanuts in the cup are counted, the blackened ones count ten apiece and the plain ones, one.

Tally is kept for each player and a suitable prize is given to the one who succeeded in securing the largest score.

PEANUT HUNT AND SCRAMBLE.

Before the guests enter the room, hide peanuts in every conceivable place, behind pictures, under chairs, on the gas fixtures, among the ornaments, five or six in vases, etc.

Give each guest a paper bag as he enters the room into which he places all the peanuts he finds. Allow a certain length of time for the hunt, then collect all the bags and select a good tall person who stands on a chair and empties the contents of each bag on the floor as fast as he can and a lively scramble for them ensues, then the one who has the greatest number of whole peanuts collected deserves a prize; the others can eat their peanuts as a comfort.

MUSICAL ILLUSTRATIONS.

A blackboard and different coloured chalk will be necessary for this game.

Give each guest a slip of paper on which is written the name of some song.

The leader announces that each one in turn steps up to the blackboard and illustrates his song in the most vivid manner possible. Each player is numbered and after No.1 finishes his drawing the others write their guesses on paper opposite his number and No.2 erases the former drawing and illustrates his song. Thus each one takes his turn, allowing time for the others to write their guesses.

When all have had their turn the correct list is read by the leader, the players checking their own lists. Prizes may be given to the one having the most correct answers and to the person who illustrated his song the most artistically.

Suggestions for songs are 'Sweet Bunch of Daisies', and 'The Four-Leaf Clover'. 'Home, Sweet Home' may be illustrated by drawing a house and a jar of sweets near it; 'America', by the outline of North America.

AN APPLE HUNT.

The hostess should prepare beforehand cards four inches square and outline on each an apple by dots concealing the outline with other dots. In one corner of the card is stuck a needle containing enough green thread to outline the apple. These 'apples' are then hidden by groups, five in a group, in different parts of the room.

A set of directions is prepared such as, No.1, 'Look under the mat'; No.2, 'Look under a certain rocking-chair', and so on. Five of these directions are sufficient, the last one telling where the apple is hidden. There are different sets of directions lettered A, B, C, etc., five in a set, all lettered alike; the group of five apples being at the end of each set of directions.

As each guest arrives he is given No.1 of some set. Following that, he finds No.2, and so on, until he finds the five apples, one of which he takes, finds the dotted apple, threads the needle and outlines it with the green cotton. The one who succeeds in finding his apple first and makes the neatest outline is the winner.

SHOUTING PROVERBS.

The more playing this game, the merrier it will be. Send one of the players from the room. The others decide upon a familiar proverb which he is to guess when he returns. Suppose the one chosen is 'A rolling stone gathers no moss.' Beginning with the leader and going to the left each player in turn takes one word, thus the leader has 'A', the next 'rolling', the next 'stone' and so on, repeating it until every player has a word. If the company is large two or three might have the same word.

When the one who was out is summoned in, he counts 1, 2, 3; when he says 3, all the players shout their word. It will be very confusing and hard to hear any one word, but after the second or third trial, one word which was heard above the rest might suggest the whole proverb.

The player who is out is given five trials in which to guess; if he does not succeed, he must go out again, but if he has listened attentively to one or two, and has guessed correctly, the player whose shouting gave away the proverb is then sent out and the game continues as before.

BAKER'S DOZEN.

This game is just for two and is similar to Tit-tat-to. Make a drawing like the illustration on the following page and the game is ready.

No.1 chooses a figure which No.2 must try to guess by indicating with a pencil dot or mark at the side of the different spaces, until he has guessed the number chosen.

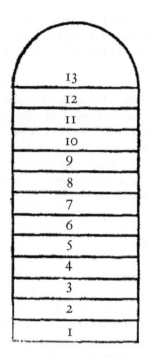

The numbers in the different spaces marked by No.2 are added to his score; and those unmarked are added to No.1.

Suppose No.1 chooses 13, and No.2 marks first 4, then 10, 9, 5, 2, and finally 13, the sum of all these (43) will be No.2's score, while the sum of the numbers unmarked (48) belongs to No.1.

The game may be played as long as is desirable, but it is more exciting to have a fixed number, such as 300 or 500.

PEANUT CONTEST.

Place two small bowls on a table at one end of the room, at the other end of the room on a table have two bags of peanuts and two knives.

The players may choose partners in any way desired. The partners play together.

The leader gives a signal, watches the time and keeps tally. When the signal is given a player, with his partner, steps to the table containing the peanuts, each takes a knife and when the leader says 'Go', each places as many peanuts as he can on the blade of the knife and carries it with one hand to the other end of the room, where he deposits the peanuts and returns for more. As many trips can be made as the time will allow. Three minutes is good time.

When the time is up the leader says, 'Stop', and the number of peanuts in each bowl is counted and accredited to the two players. Each pair takes turn in playing, time and tally being kept for each until all have played.

The list of contestants is read aloud, the partners who succeeded in carrying the greatest number of peanuts to their bowls receive a prize.

DEFINITIONS.

Provide each player with pencil and paper. The leader has a dictionary which she opens at any place and selects a word which the rest are to define.

The players write the word and their definition of it on the slips of paper. When the leader taps a bell all the slips must be collected and mixed up in a basket or hat.

Each player then draws out a slip and the definitions are read aloud in turn. The leader decides which one has written a definition most like the one in the dictionary. The author of the best one rises, receives the dictionary, gives out a word and the game proceeds as before.

ALPHABETICAL ANSWERS.

Prepare cards with one letter of the alphabet on each, omitting V, X, Z. Of course if the company is large, several will have the same letter.

The cards are pinned on the guests, and it is announced that no one must answer any question presented to him except by a sentence commencing with the letter on his card, the answer being given before the questioner could count ten.

No two players can question a person at the same time, and no one can give the same answer twice.

If a player begins his reply with a wrong letter or does not answer in time, his letter is taken from him by his questioner, who adds it to his and he then has the privilege of answering with either of his letters.

The player who is without a card is supplied with one again but after the third trial he is out of the game.

PITCH BASKET.

Select a number of small fruit baskets, all the same size, and have a box of checkers handy. Suppose you have five, on the bottom of one mark 20, on another 15, on two, 5; and on the other, 0. Place the baskets in a row on the floor so their numbers cannot be seen.

Choose sides, giving the red checkers to the leader of one side and the black checkers to the other. One side lines up about 10ft away from the baskets, the leader giving each player a checker; if there are any left he keeps them and has the privilege of throwing them. Each one in turn throws his checker into any basket, trusting to luck that they fall into a basket with a number on it.

When all have played the leader turns up each basket to see its number and counts the number of checkers thrown into it. If there were two in basket No.20, it would count 40; if three in one basket No.5, it would be 15; if four in the other basket No.5, 20; and if there were three in basket 0, it would count nothing. Thus the score for that side is 75. The players on the other side line up and play as the others did. The order of the baskets must be changed by someone not of that side, so no one knows which is which. Their score is added up.

The game continues until a certain number, 300 or 500, has been reached. The side scoring that number of points first is victorious.

WHO AM I?

As the guests arrive pin a card with a name of some noted author, politician, or poet written on it, on their backs, so that everyone can see it but themselves.

Of course, each person wants to know who he is, so the guests talk to each other as though they were the person whose name is on the other's back, but do not mention the name, and from the conversation, they have to guess who they are.

PROGRESSIVE PUZZLES.

The players are provided with pasteboard cards two inches square, and scissors. At a signal, given by the hostess, they must cut their cards in four pieces, the cuts must intersect in some place, but the card can be cut in any other way.

When the cards are cut and the four pieces mixed, they are passed to the player at the right, who has to put the four pieces together correctly.

A certain time is given for each puzzle and each time it is passed to the right, until each player has his own puzzle again.

TIT FOR TAT.

Plan to have an even number of guests invited, half ladies and half gentlemen.

Provide thick boards for each lady, also a hammer and paper of tacks, and for the men, plain hats (untrimmed) and material for trimming, also a paper of pins.

When all the guests arrive set them to work. The ladies have to hammer as many tacks in straight in their boards as they can, during the allotted time, while the men trim their hats, choosing their material from that which is provided. When the time (which may be as long or as short as you wish) is up, the men put on their respective hats and pass before the ladies for inspection; the one having the best trimmed one receives a prize.

The men inspect the work of the ladies, and the one who has hammered the most tacks into her board 'straight', receives a prize.

EYE–GUESSING.

Hang a sheet or screen in a doorway between two rooms and cut six holes, the size and shape of eyes, each pair a distance apart, in it, some up high and some down low.

Choose groups of four to go behind the sheet, the rest of the guests staying in the other room.

Three of the chosen four look through the holes at a time. The short ones can stand on chairs and look through the high pair, while the tall ones can stoop down, thus confusing those who have to guess who the pairs of eyes belong to.

A short time is given for guessing each group, and then the next set go out.

The guesses are written on slips of paper and after all the eyes have been 'examined', the correct list is read by one who stayed behind the sheet all the time.

THE PRINCE OF WALES.

Any number can play this game. The players stand in a line around the room and number themselves, beginning with one, until each has a number.

The leader, who has no number and who has charge of the game, begins by saying –

The Prince of Wales has lost his hat, all on account of No.1, Sir;

then No.1 says:

No, sir, not I, sir, No.5, [or any number he wishes], sir.

Then No.5, repeats what No.1 said, giving another number instead of 5; but if he fails to respond, then the leader says,

No.5 to the foot, sir,

and then all those who were below No.5 move up one, and thus their number becomes one less.

The leader begins again and he must be very quick to send those to the foot, who fail to respond.

COMMERCE.

The guests are seated around a table, each one having a pile of fifty beans in front of him. The leader has two packs of playing cards, one of which is used for an auction sale, one card at a time being sold to the highest bidder, who pays for it in beans.

When all the cards of the first pack have been sold, the players arrange their cards and beans on the table ready for business.

The auctioneer then holds up the second pack and announces that he will call the cards off one at a time, and as he does so, the player who has the duplicate of that card must give it up to the auctioneer.

After each calling there is a little time allowed to buy or sell the cards, the object of the game being either to have more beans than anyone else, or to have the duplicate card which is at the bottom of the second pack, thus causing a very exciting time as the second pile diminishes.

LAUGH A LITTLE.

The players sit in a circle with one in the middle for leader. The leader must be one who laughs heartily and is very quick.

He begins the game by throwing a plain, white handkerchief up in the air, as high as he can, and while it is in the air, everyone must laugh, but the minute it touches the floor, there must be perfect silence. The leader must catch those who are still laughing and send them from the ring.

The game goes on until everyone is out of the circle. If there should happen to be one who doesn't laugh when the handkerchief is on the floor, he surely deserves a prize.

LOCATION.

Choose two leaders who select sides. One begins by calling the name of some town or place and then counts ten. While he is counting, the opposite opponent must answer where the place is. If he fails to answer before ten is counted, he must drop out.

Then the leader of the other side takes his turn, and challenges some player of the opposite side.

The side which stands up the longest, wins the game.

FASHION NOTES.

The names of various fashion papers, such as *The Delineator*, *The Styles*, *Le Bon Ton*, *Ladies' Home Journal*, are written on cards, which are cut so that it requires the two parts to know what the title is. Distribute these among the guests, who hunt for the corresponding part, thus getting their partners; crayon and paper is given out and the ladies are requested to draw and colour a gown representing the one she has on, while the men are asked to write a description of the gown.

The drawings and descriptions are collected after time is allowed, and placed on a table for display.

Prizes may be awarded to the partners having the best drawing and description.

STRAY SYLLABLES.

Prepare long strips of paper on which the guests are requested to write several words of three or more syllables, leaving spaces between each syllable.

When this is done, cut up the words into the syllables and mix thoroughly. Then each player draws three syllables and tries to construct a word.

If a word can't be made of all three syllables, maybe it can be made of two, but if it is then impossible to construct a word, the player must wait until the rest draw three syllables again, and perchance he may be able to construct two words, using the syllables he could not use before.

The one constructing the most words, wins the game.

QUAKER MEETING.

All the guests sit in a circle and the leader begins by saying: 'This is a very solemn occasion.' He then twirls his thumbs and looks very solemn. Commencing with the player to the right of the leader, each one in turn repeats what he has said, very solemnly twirls his thumbs, and keeps twirling them, until each one has repeated it, and it is the leader's turn again.

He then says, 'Sister Jane died last night', still twirling his thumbs. This goes around the circle as before. Then the player to the right of the leader says, 'How did she die?' and he replies, 'Like this', moving his right hand up and down. Thus each one tells his neighbour, and makes the motion just as the leader has done.

After each one has said this, still repeating the same question and answer, the leader moves his left hand up and down, too, thus both hands are going; the next time both hands and the right foot are moving; then both hands and both feet; next, hands, feet, and head, bobbing up and down; last, fall back in the chair uttering a hideous groan as if dead.

No one must laugh during the whole game; whoever does, must leave the circle.

MAGIC MUSIC.

One player is sent from the room and the rest decide upon something he must do when called in.

When this has been done he is summoned by magic music which is made by having one of the players strike on something which will make a noise. If there is a piano, so much the better, if not, a piece of metal or a bell will do.

As he nears the object which he is to find the music grows very loud, and faint when he is far away.

Suppose he is to take a flower from a vase, and give it to one of the players. As he nears the flowers, the music grows louder and louder, and if he touches one, it stops; then he knows he has to do something with it. If he smells it, the music grows faint, and he knows he is wrong. As he starts to give it to the players, the music varies until he has given it to the right one.

Someone else then leaves the room, and the game goes on as before.

PATCHWORK ILLUSTRATIONS.

For this game it is necessary for the hostess to collect a large number of pictures from magazines, advertisement pages or papers. These are placed in the centre of a table around which the players are seated.

Each guest is provided with a paper at the top of which is written a quotation. The hostess announces that each player is to illustrate his or her quotation with the pictures provided. The pictures are pasted on the papers, and if necessary, a background can be made with pencil or pen and ink.

The papers are then arranged on a table for inspection and a prize is awarded for the best illustration.

BIOGRAPHY.

Provide the players with pencil and paper. The leader then announces that a biography is to be written, and the first thing to write is the name of some person in the room; the paper is folded over so the name cannot be seen and passed to the player at his left, who writes a date which is the birth date, and the name of some town; the paper is folded again and passed to the left and this time a sentence of ten words is written about early childhood – from one to ten years. Next, a sentence of same length telling of events between twenty and forty years; next, between forty and fifty years; date of death next, last, remark about this life. When all has been written, the folded papers are passed to the left again and each player reads his paper aloud.

The more ridiculous the sentences, the better the biography, and as no one knows what is under the folded parts, sometimes the date of death will be earlier than that of birth, or there will be a vast difference in time.

Example – Name, John Smith. Born 4 July 1449, London. From one to ten years, mischievous child, quarrelled with everybody, expelled from school, stole eggs.

From twenty to forty, stayed home, did dressmaking, became sickly, remained an old maid.

From forty to fifty, became a wealthy widower, left with three children to raise. Died 1 January 1860. Most remarkable man that ever lived in his little town.

ORCHESTRA.

Any number can play this game, the more the merrier. Each player is told to play some imaginary instrument. The leader with an imaginary baton, begins by humming some lively, familiar tune. The players follow with motions suitable to their instruments and sing the tune the leader is humming.

When the leader pretends to play some instrument, the player who has that imaginary instrument, must pretend he is leader and beat time with the baton, but as soon as the real leader changes the instrument or beats time again the player must continue with his own instrument.

The leader must be quick to change from one instrument to another and the players must be quick to follow him, for if they don't, they have to leave the orchestra until the piece is over.

WHO IS MY NEXT-DOOR NEIGHBOUR?

Half of the company are blindfolded. They are led to a row of chairs arranged in the middle of the room, each sitting so there is a vacant chair behind him.

The other half, who are not blindfolded, very quietly take the vacant chairs and sit perfectly still.

The leader then announces that those not blindfolded are to sing when he gives the signal, and the blindfolded ones, who are to remain still, must listen attentively to their right-hand neighbour and guess who he is.

Some familiar tunes must be chosen and the singers can disguise their voices if they choose. The leader begins by playing the tune on the piano and when he says 'sing', the victim singers begin while the blind victims listen.

One verse of the song will be enough for this medley and those whose voices have been recognised, exchange places with the blindfolded ones, while the others remain in the same place until the listener has guessed who he is. The game then goes on as before.

FIRE.

Choose two leaders from among the players. Each leader chooses his side. The sides sit opposite each other, the leader of one throws a ball to anyone in the opposite side. As he does he says either, 'earth', 'air', 'water', or 'fire', and counts ten.

The person who caught the ball must answer before he finishes counting ten. If 'earth' was called he must name some quadruped found therein; if 'water', some fish must be named, or 'air', the name of some bird; but if 'fire' was called he must remain perfectly still.

If the players give a wrong answer or speak when they should be silent they are out, and the leader must throw the ball to someone else, but if the players answer correctly, it is their turn to throw the ball to someone in the opposite side, and the game goes on as before. The side whose players stand up the longest, wins the game.

THE MONTHS.

The leader need be the only one who understands this game. He asks, 'What month are you going away in?' One player might answer 'September'. He then asks, 'What will you wear?' 'What will you take with you?' and 'What will you do?' All the answers must be given with the initial letter of the month chosen. For instance, the answers to the above questions may be: 1st, 'Silk stockings', 2nd, 'Sardine sandwiches', 3rd, 'See the sights.'

The answers will probably be mixed as the players do not know the trick. Each one who misses pays a forfeit, and the leader questions the next player. When one or two do catch on, the more ridiculous they make their answers, the funnier the game.

BELL BUFF.

In this game all the players except one are blindfolded. This one is called the guide and has a small bell which he rings during the game.

All the blind men are led to one end of the room by the guide. He then takes his position a little distance from them and rings the bell, which is the signal for the game to begin.

The blind men grope around wildly for their guide who rings the bell all the time, but must move in different places, so as to escape the blind men who are hunting him. The blind men are only guided by the sound of the bell, and the guide must be very quick to change his positions or he will be caught by his pursuers.

The first blind man who catches the guide, exchanges places with him, and the game goes on as before.

POSTMAN.

The players sit in a circle; one is chosen for 'postman', is blindfolded, and another is chosen for Postmaster.

The Postmaster gives each player the name of some city or town, and stands outside the ring so he can give orders.

The 'postman' stands inside the circle and when the Postmaster says, 'I have sent a letter from London to Birmingham', the players having these names must exchange places, and he must try to capture one. If he succeeds he takes that one's place, the one caught then becoming 'postman'.

The Postmaster must exchange names very rapidly, and if a player should remain seated when his city is called, he has to be 'postman'.

If the Postmaster says, 'general delivery', all exchange places, and the 'postman' tries to secure a vacant place.

SPOONEY FUN.

All the players sit in a circle. One is chosen to be out. He is blindfolded and given a spoon (a large one) with which he is to feel. He stands in the middle of the circle, then is turned around three times and told to guess who the first person, which he touches with the spoon, is.

He advances cautiously until he touches someone. Then with the back of the spoon he feels the person all over. The players must keep perfectly quiet, disguising themselves if they see fit, as the collars and cuffs of the men will be felt very easily with the spoon.

As soon as the blindfolded one has guessed who the player is he was feeling, they exchange places and the game goes on as before, but if he fails to guess the first time, or has felt with his hand instead of the spoon he is out again and remains out, until he has guessed correctly.

CITIES.

Provide all the guests with pencil and paper. The hostess then requests that each write the name of the city in which he was born, and under that a sentence, descriptive of that city or containing something suggestive of it. The letters of the city form the words of the sentence and must follow in regular order.

Allow fifteen minutes for composing the sentences, then collect them, mix them up, and each player is given one. Thus each one has some other person's slip to read. The one who composed the best sentences deserves a prize.

Examples:

City – London.
Sentence – L-oud O-n N-oisy D-ays O-f N-otoriety

City – Leeds.
Sentence – L-ovely E-venings, E-ven D-ays S-hine

GOING TO CHINA.

This is a catch game for those who have never played it. The leader begins by saying, 'I'm going to sail for China next week, I would like to have you go, what will you take?' This question is asked of every player and there are many different answers, but all cannot go, as they have not answered correctly.

The point is, if you wish to go sailing, you must take something which commences with the same letter as the initial of your last name. The leader then says, 'You can go.'

For example, suppose the player who is asked the question says she will take bananas. If her last name begins with B she can go, but if not, the leader says, 'Lou cannot go this trip.'

The game continues until everyone has guessed the trick and they can all go.

A PENNY FOR YOUR THOUGHTS.

Provide each player with pencil and paper and a penny. The hostess explains that the answers to the following questions are things which are found on every penny.

The questions may either be written on the paper beforehand or the guests can write them as the hostess asks them. A prize may be awarded to the player whose paper contains the greatest number of correct answers.

1. An emblem of victory, (laurel wreath).
2. An emblem of royalty, (crown).
3. A South American fruit, (date).
4. A spring flower, (tulips, two lips).
5. A portion of a hill, (brow).
6. A portion of a river, (mouth).
7. A messenger, (one cent, sent).
8. A piece of armour, (shield).
9. Mode of ancient punishment, (stripes).
10. Means of inflicting it, (lashes).
11. Something to be found in school, (pupil).
12. Three weapons, (three arrows).
13. An animal, (hare, hair).
14. A part of a stove, (lid).
15. Plenty of assurance, (cheek).

16. The first American settler, (Indian).
17. Part of a duck, (feathers).
18. A place of worship, (temple).
19. Two sides of a vote, (eyes and nose, ayes and noes).
20. The cry of victory, (won, one).

MISQUOTED QUOTATIONS.

Choose very familiar quotations from Longfellow, Shakespeare, Tennyson, or any well-known author or poet, and write them on slips of paper.

Change some of the words of the original, or even a whole line, and when each guest receives his slip he is requested to repeat the quotation correctly.

For example – 'To be, or not to be; that is the question', may be written, 'To be, or not to be: that is the problem'.

LITERARY SALAD.

Salad leaves are prepared for this game by folding and twisting pieces of green tissue paper until they look like lettuce leaves. Then paste slips of white paper containing a quotation, on each leaf.

The participants of this salad are requested to guess the name of the author of their quotation. This may be played very easily at a church social where the leaves may contain Bible verses instead of quotations, and the players are asked to tell just where their verses are found, in what book and chapter.

BROKEN QUOTATIONS.

This is a good game to play at the beginning of a social gathering, as the guests have to mingle together and thus become better acquainted, and the stiffness of a formal gathering passes off.

The hostess has prepared familiar quotations which were written on paper and then cut in two or three parts and pinned in different places around the room.

The guests are requested to find as many quotations as they can during a certain length of time.

As the parts are scattered all over the room, it isn't as easy as it sounds to find the complete quotations. The person gathering the most quotations, deserves a prize.

PARCEL DELIVERY.

Packages of all shapes and sizes and securely wrapped up are prepared by the hostess who has numbered each one. The players are provided with pencil and slips of paper with numbers corresponding to the numbers on the parcels, arranged down one side.

The guests sit in a circle and the packages are passed from one to the other. Each one is allowed to feel the packages as much as he pleases, but no one must look inside.

As the packages are passed, the names, guessed by the sense of touch, are written opposite their appropriate numbers on the slips of paper.

After all the bundles have been passed, the hostess opens each one and keeps account of those who have guessed correctly, while those who have failed, are requested to read their guesses as this affords much amusement.

WHO ARE THEY?

Photographs of noted people, labelled with names that do not belong to them, are hung about the room. Each picture is numbered.

The guests, provided with pencil and paper, are given a certain length of time in which to guess the correct names, which are written opposite their corresponding numbers.

Familiar photographs such as Dickens, Shakespeare, Napoleon, etc., should be chosen.

SWAPS.

The guests are requested to bring something wrapped up in paper, which they wish to get rid of.

The hostess prepares a duplicate set of numbers, pinning one number on each parcel, as the guests pass by her. When she gives a signal (clapping hands or ringing a bell), the two persons having No. 1 pinned on their packages exchange them, those having No.2, and so on, until all have exchanged or swapped. Then all open their packages, some may have received better things, while others may have a worse swap.

TALKING SHOP.

Partners may be chosen for this game by writing names referring to ladies on one set of papers like, 'Judy', 'Jill', 'Juliet', and names referring to men on another set of papers like, 'Punch', 'Jack', 'Romeo'. Hand each guest a slip of paper with the name on it and each one hunts for his partner.

When all the partners are found, the leader announces that at a given signal all the ladies are to talk to their partners for five minutes about household affairs, shopping, or fashions. Each man listens attentively to his partner, and when the five minutes are up, he has to write a short account of her conversation, on paper, which the hostess provides. Five minutes is allowed for this.

Then the men talk to the ladies for five minutes about business affairs, stocks, law, building or medicine, and it is the ladies' turn to write a short composition of what she heard.

The papers are collected, the hostess reads them, and a prize is awarded to the best or most amusing account.

SIGHT UNSEEN.

Partners may be chosen in any way for this game. The host gives each pair a sheet of paper and pencil. The partners decide among themselves which one is the best artist, he or she (as the case may be) takes the pencil and paper, while the other receives some common object from the host.

The chairs must be arranged side by side, but facing in opposite directions, so the one who is to draw may not see the object his partner has. When the signal is given to begin, the one having the object describes it to his partner, who must draw it, from the description given.

After twenty minutes have passed, the drawings and their objects are collected, arranged side by side, and it is decided by vote which drawing is most like the object it represents.

A STUDY IN ZOOLOGY.

It will be necessary to have several sheets of silhouette paper (black on one side and white on the other), a large sheet of white cardboard, several pairs of scissors, and as many pencils as there are players, for this game.

Each player is handed a piece of silhouette paper, on the white side of which is written a number and the name of some animal. The players are handed pencils and requested to draw the animal, assigned to each, on the white side of the paper. The animals are then cut out and handed to the hostess. Fifteen minutes are allowed for this.

The hostess, having collected all the animals, pastes them back side out, on the sheet of cardboard, and writes a number corresponding to the one already on the animal, underneath each. The cardboard sheet is hung up where all can see and the players are handed pieces of paper with numbers arranged down one side, on which each player is to write opposite its corresponding number what each animal is supposed to represent.

A prize may be given to the one guessing the greatest number of animals correctly.

AUCTION SALE.

Provide twenty or more bundles, all shapes and sizes, securely wrapped. Each bundle has a name on it suggestive of what is inside. For instance, 'A pair of kids', may contain two kid hair curlers, 'A bunch of dates', may be a calendar; 'A diamond pin', a dime and a pin.

Each guest is given a bag containing fifty beans, no one can bid higher than fifty.

The auctioneer, who must be a witty person, who can carry on a lively bidding, stands by a table where the parcels are piled and carries on the sale until all the parcels are sold. The bundles are then opened by the purchasers and there is much merriment over the contents.

THE GENTEEL LADY.

The players sit in a circle. The leader begins by saying, 'I, a genteel lady [or gentleman, as the case may be] always genteel, come to you, a genteel lady [or gentleman] always genteel [bows to the player on the right], from yonder genteel lady [or gentleman] always genteel [bows to player on left], to tell you that she has an eagle.'

The next player repeats that word for word and adds something about the eagle, for instance, the last part may be, 'to tell you that she has an eagle with silver beak.' The next player may add, 'golden claws', the next 'emerald eyes', the next 'purple feathers', and so on.

The players who repeat every word correctly, adding their description of the eagle, remain 'genteel', but those who make a mistake become 'horned' instead of 'genteel'.

The leader has charge of the 'horns' which may be toothpicks or pieces of paper twisted up tight. For every mistake a 'horn' is tucked in the player's hair. Each player repeats what the leader has said, but if the player next to him is 'horned', he must substitute 'horned' for 'genteel' when referring to him.

When each one has repeated this tale, the players who have 'horns', and there will be many, must pay a forfeit for every 'horn' they have.

RHYMES.

Provide each player with slips of paper and pencil. The hostess then announces that each one is to write some question at the top of the paper, fold the paper over and pass it to the player at the left, who writes a noun, folds the paper over and passes it to the left again.

The players who then receive the slips are requested to write one or more stanzas of poetry containing the noun and question written at the top of the paper.

Allow fifteen minutes for this, then pass the papers to the left and they are then read in turn. A prize may be given to the one who wrote the best poetry.

Examples –

Question – Where did you get that hat?
Noun – Fair.

'Where did you get that hat?'
Said Shortie to Mr Fat,
'I stole it from the Fair,
When I was leaving there.'

Question – Can you dance?
Noun – Day.

'May-day! let us away!
Can you dance?
Here's your chance,
On this lovely May-day.'

ART GALLERY.

Select copies of famous paintings, those familiar to everyone, and hang them around the room.

Neither the name of the painting nor of the artist must be on it, only a number on each picture.

Provide the guests with pencil and paper and allow a certain length of time, according to the number of pictures, for guessing the names and artists.

HUNTING FOR BOOK TITLES.

The hostess must prepare beforehand pictures, cut from magazine advertisements and miscellaneous articles, suggestive of the titles of books.

These are arranged around the room, some on tables, some on the wall, and in any place, so all the guests can see them. All the articles are numbered.

The guests are handed pencil and paper and the hostess announces that all the articles represent the title of some book and when guessed the names are to be written opposite their corresponding numbers. Allow half an hour for the hunt, and when the time is up the hostess reads the correct list and the player who has guessed the largest number correctly, deserves a prize.

Examples – A large bow of orange ribbon pinned on a curtain, immediately suggests 'A Bow of Orange Ribbon', by Amelia Barr. A picture of several boys suggests 'Little Men', by Louisa M. Alcott. A picture of General Grant cut in half suggests 'Half a Hero'.

PART III

Games for Special Days

JACK FROST.

Around Christmas and New Year's the children will enjoy playing this. All form a circle; one, Jack Frost, stands in the middle.

Jack Frost runs around inside the circle and touches one child on her right hand, and goes back to his place again. The child touched says: 'Jack Frost came this way', the child to her left says: 'What did he do?' No.1 says: 'He nipped my right hand', (shaking her right hand). No.2 tells No.3 about Jack Frost, each doing as No.1 did, and thus it goes down the circle, until back to No.1 again.

Jack Frost then steps out and bites her left hand, and now both hands are shaking; thus each time Jack Frost nips some part, that is shaking with the rest, until the children are hopping up and down, and shaking all over.

MAGIC CANDLES.

Arrange twelve candles, one for each month, in a row about two feet apart. Have the candles different colours suggestive of the months they represent, such as, green for March and red for December.

The children form in line and one at a time jump over the candles, which are lighted.

If a light goes out the child who has just jumped will have bad luck in that month which the candle represents.

THE LUCKY OR UNLUCKY SLIPPER.

A slipper is waved three times over the head and then thrown on the floor.

If the toe be toward the player, good luck is coming. If the heel, bad luck is in store, and if it rests on its side, there is hope for something better.

CAKES.

On 6 January, Twelfth Night was celebrated in the olden times. Then all the pastry cooks did their finest baking and decked their windows with marvellous productions of cakes.

If a party is being planned for this day invite your guests to come dressed as cakes. Just the ladies will do this and the men can wear miniature cooking utensils if they choose.

Give each lady a number and each man a pencil and slip of paper. The men must guess what cakes the ladies represent and write their answers with the corresponding numbers on the paper.

When all the cakes have been guessed the correct list is read by the hostess and the one having the largest number of correct answers may be awarded a prize.

A prize may also be awarded to the lady attired in the best representation. One dressed in dark brown would suggest 'chocolate cake'; another in orange-coloured cheesecloth, 'orange cake'; another with wreaths of raisins, currants and citron, suggest 'fruit cake'; while one in just a plain dress with no signs suggestive of any cake may be 'lady cake'; another carrying a hammer and pounding it whenever she saw fit, suggests 'pound cake'.

VALENTINES.

When inviting the guests for a Valentine party, request each one to bring an original valentine addressed to one of the guests. As the guests arrive, the hostess collects the valentines, being careful to keep those addressed to ladies in one pile, and those addressed to gentlemen in another.

The hostess then hands each one a valentine, giving the gentlemen those addressed to the ladies and the ladies those for the gentlemen. The valentines are then read aloud and a jolly time will be the result.

A prize may be awarded for the best valentine, the brightest and most witty.

INITIAL COMPLIMENTS.

Each gentleman is handed a slip of paper with the name of a lady guest on it. The gentlemen are then requested, one at a time, to go to their respective ladies, giving each a compliment, every word of which begins with the initial letter of the lady's first name.

As each lady is addressed by a gentleman, she replies, using the initial letter of his name in her answer.

Votes are taken as to the best compliment and answer and a simple prize may be awarded the pair who obtained the most votes.

HEART HUNT.

Cut out of red, white, blue, yellow and green paper hearts of all shapes and sizes, then cut each heart into four pieces and scatter these all over the room, on the floor, chairs, tables, behind pictures, etc.

Allow a certain length of time for the hunt, and when all the pieces have been collected, request each guest to put his pieces together and see how many whole hearts of the same colour he has collected.

The white heart counts 1; the blue, 2; the yellow, 3; the green, 4; and the red, 5. The one scoring the greatest number of points is the winner of hearts and deserves a prize. A booby prize may be awarded the one who has only broken hearts.

HEART PRICKS.

A large heart made of some red material, (flannel or cheesecloth) is pinned securely to a sheet, which may be stretched on the wall or door. In the centre of the large red heart is a small white heart, either sewed or pinned on.

Each guest is given an arrow of white cloth with a pin in one end. When everything is ready the hostess blindfolds the guests one at a time, and standing a certain distance from the heart, starts them in the right direction.

Each one endeavours to pin his arrow on the heart; the one pinning it nearest to the middle of the white heart wins the game.

VALENTINE PUZZLE.

Select five good paper valentines. Paste each on a piece of cardboard and cut into small pieces. Have five small tables in the room and place a puzzle on each. If the company is small, assign five persons to a table, if larger, use your own judgment.

Each one at the table takes his turn, trying to put the valentine together in its proper shape. Each player is timed, and the one who succeeds in putting it together in the shortest time is the winner.

If desired, the players can go from one table to the other; the one who succeeds in putting the most puzzles together out of the five, is the winner.

HEARTS AND MITTENS.

Cut out of red cardboard half as many hearts and mittens as you expect in your company. Out of blue cardboard cut hearts and mittens for the rest of the company. Number them so every heart has its corresponding mitten. Attach strings or ribbons to each and place them in a basket.

Each guest takes the end of a string and pulls out his heart or mitten, as the case may be. Each one then hunts for his partner.

When all are paired off, a circle is formed and someone strikes up a lively march. Whenever the music stops, all the ladies stand still, and the gentlemen move up one. This goes on until everyone has had a different partner, and finally, when the original one comes, there is a grand march before the circle breaks up.

RIVEN HEARTS.

Another way of securing partners for the evening is as follows: suspend two large hearts made of either white or red paper from the ceiling, several feet apart. Make a hole in each, through which are hung the ends of long strings. The ladies hold the strings on one side and the gentlemen on the other.

When the hostess gives a signal, all pull on their strings. Thus the hearts are riven and partners are found holding the ends of the same string.

PROPOSALS.

As the guests assemble for the Valentine party, give each gentleman a slip of paper bearing the name of a woman, and the ladies, the name of some man, noted in fiction as lovers. Thus the one who has Romeo hunts for the lady who has Juliet on her paper.

When all know who their partners are, the ladies must evade every attempt on the part of the gentlemen of proposing to them during the evening.

A prize is given to the gentleman who has succeeded in proposing, and to the girl who has alluded all efforts of her partner by her wit and ingenuity.

Another way is to have the proposals progressive. Every gentleman must propose to every lady before the evening is over. The ladies use every effort they can to prevent them from 'coming to the point'. The man making the most offers receives the prize. The lady receiving the fewest declarations receives a prize.

APRIL FIRST.

For an April Fool's Day gathering, ask each guest to come prepared to do some sleight of hand trick. When all are assembled, each one in turn performs his trick. A vote is taken for the most clever and a prize is awarded.

Each one present endeavours to fool someone else during the evening. The one who has not been fooled once during the whole evening receives a prize; the one who is fooled the most times is given a prize, too.

EASTER EGG RACE.

Colour an even number of eggs, half the number one colour, the other half, another. Place all the eggs of one colour on the floor in a line at intervals of one foot. At the end of the line put a basket. Form a similar line, a little distance from the other, of the remaining eggs. For convenience, we will say one line is of green eggs, the other of pink.

Choose two players as leaders, who select their sides. One side chooses the green row, and the other, the pink. Two, one player from each side, play at a time.

When all is ready the two leaders stand by their respective rows, each is given a large spoon, and when told to 'Go', each one spoons up the eggs, one at a time, and carries them to the basket at the end of the line. The one who succeeds in spooning up all his eggs first wins for his side.

Thus each player in turn works for his side until all have had a chance and the side whose players were the most successful is the winning side.

SUSPENDED EGGS.

After an egg hunt, several eggs may be gathered together and a string or ribbon run through each and hung in different lengths from a chandelier. Candy eggs and little baskets of eggs may be suspended, too. Place a tablecloth or sheet underneath to prevent the carpet from being spoiled by the downfall.

Each child in turn is blindfolded and given a cane with which to strike the suspended eggs. Whatever is knocked down is his. If he fails to knock something down the first time, he may have another turn.

EGG RACE.

Give each child a tablespoon and a hard-boiled egg. The children form in line and one is the leader. Each one holds the spoon with the egg in its bowl at arm's length and hops on one foot, following wherever the leader leads them.

The leader may take them up stairs, over stools, and any place hard to reach on one foot. To drop the egg or rest on both feet prevents one from continuing in the game. She must stay out until the next time round.

ROLLING EGGS.

Mark on the table, or on the floor, if preferred, with chalk, four parallel lines, eight or ten feet long, and four or five inches apart. Thus there are three narrow spaces. At the end of each space make a circle, numbering the middle one 10, and the other two, 5. The middle space is marked 3, and the other two, 1.

The object of the game is to have each child roll five eggs, one at a time, down the middle space to the circles at the ends. If the egg goes into the middle circle, it counts 10, but if it stops in the middle space, it counts only 3, and so on, counting the number of the place where it stops.

Tally is kept for each child, the one scoring the most points wins the game.

BUNNY'S EGG.

On a sheet draw a rough sketch of a good-sized rabbit, the regular Easter bunny, standing on its hind legs, and holding its paws as if it were carrying an egg.

Stretch the sheet on the wall and tack it firmly in place. Cut eggs out of different coloured cloth to represent Easter eggs. The eggs should be as large as the space between the rabbit's paws. In each egg stick a pin.

Blindfold the children in turn and give each an egg, which is to be pinned on the sheet, and right in 'Bunny's' arms, if possible.

As the children take their turn, no matter how straight on the way they were started, 'Bunny' will be surrounded with eggs, until some child pins the egg in his arms. This child deserves a prize.

GUY FAWKES' NIGHT.

Aside from the enjoyment of firecrackers, etc., there are a few games to amuse the children on this day. If a party has been planned, the rooms should be appropriately decorated for the occasion.

As soon as all the children arrive choose two leaders, who in turn select sides. A line is marked on the floor and the sides stand on each side of this boundary line. A few feet from the line on each side is placed a flag. Any flag can be made to stand up by placing the end of the stick securely in the hole of an empty spool. Each leader guards his own flag.

The children endeavour to secure their opponents' flag. If a leader tags anyone who crosses the boundary and comes too near the flag, that child is out of the game. However, if one does succeed in capturing the other's flag, and carries it over the boundary into his side, that side is victorious.

FLAGS OF ALL NATIONS.

Flags of all nations are collected and displayed around the room. Each one is numbered. The guests are given pencil and paper with numbers down the left-hand side.

Opposite each number the guest writes the names of the country which the flag bearing the corresponding number stands for. Allow a certain length of time for guessing, then collect the papers, read the correct list, and correct the papers. Prizes may be awarded, but the satisfaction of having guessed the most seems to be enough reward.

OUR FLAG.

Each child is given a piece of white paper or cardboard 6½ by 3½ inches in size. All sit around a table on which is placed red and blue paper by each one's place. Scissors and a bottle of mucilage are handy. The children are given a certain length of time in which to make their flags, putting the blue and red strips correctly on their pieces of cardboard. The one who completes his flag first deserves a prize.

Suspend a bell in a doorway low enough for the children to reach. The children stand about ten feet away and each in turn throws a beanbag, endeavoring to make the bell ring. Those who succeed in making it ring receive little bells as a reward.

The contents of several boxes of torpedoes may be emptied and hidden around the room. The children hunt for them, and have a jolly time shooting them off after the hunt is over.

HALLOWE'EN.

A Hallowe'en party is probably the only gathering where the stiffness and formality entirely disappear. Everyone is in for a good time, and should be dressed in old clothes ready to try all sorts of experiments.

Decorate the room appropriately with pumpkin jack-o'-lanterns, greens, weird lights, and strings of peppers, if possible. Mirrors should be in profusion. Effective lights may be made from cucumbers by scraping out the inside and cutting holes in the rind for eyes and nose, and placing a candle in each.

Persons dressed as ghosts may receive the guests and usher them into the room where the fun is to be. As soon as a person enters, the hostess, who is not a ghost, blindfolds the victim, and those already in the room take turns shaking hands with him. He has to guess who each person is. It is marvellous how many mistakes will be made, even if the guests are the best of friends.

HALLOWE'EN STORIES.

There are several ways of telling ghastly stories on Hallowe'en. Have a large ball of different coloured yarn handy and before the midnight hour, turn out the lights, and ask all the players to sit in a circle. The hostess, holding the ball of yarn, begins by telling some weird story, unwinding the yarn as she proceeds, until she comes to a different colour, and then she tosses the ball to someone in the circle, and that one must proceed with the story until she comes to a different colour. It is then tossed to another, and so on, until the ball is unwound and the story ended.

Another way, more ghastly still, is to give each guest a saucer in which is a handful of salt and some alcohol. Each one in turn lights the contents of the saucer and tells some ghost story, continuing until all the alcohol is burned, and no longer. The stories may be lively or sad.

HALLOWE'EN FATES.

For obtaining partners, fill a pumpkin rind with nuts, which have been opened, had the meat taken out, some token of the fate placed inside, and glued together again with a ribbon attached to each. Those drawing nuts having the same coloured ribbon are partners. The one whose nut has a ring in, is to be married next; if a coin, he is to be the most wealthy; if a thimble, a spinster all her life. The other nuts may have slips of paper with prophecies written on them.

A bag filled with nuts may be tied up tightly and hung in a doorway. One of the players is blindfolded and given a stick with which he is to hit the bag as hard as he can, thus breaking it, and scattering the nuts on the floor. The one who succeeds in gathering the greatest number of nuts will be the luckiest during the year.

Fill two large pans with sawdust. Bury in one pan pieces of paper bearing a rhyme about one's future, these can be about the ladies for the men to draw, and in the other pan verses for the ladies to draw. The papers are folded up tightly. The ladies and gentlemen take turns putting in their thumbs. As soon as a verse is found it is read aloud.

Example for the men to draw:

Medium height, eyes of blue,
Charming girl is awaiting you.

For the ladies:

Tall and slight, with red hair,
Fond of walking and fresh air.

SOME MORE FATES.

In addition to the regulation 'bobbing for apples', 'floating needles' and throwing the apple peel over the head, there are many other amusements of prophecy.

In a doorway a portiere of apples may be hung. Apples are strung on strings of various lengths. The tallest guests endeavour to bite those swinging on the longest strings stooping in the attempt, while the shorter ones reach for those above. The one who succeeds in eating the whole of his apple just by biting it, will never want for anything.

A horseshoe is hung in a doorway. Each guest is given three small apples. Each in turn tries to throw the apples, one at a time, through the horseshoe. If he succeeds in sending all three through, he will always be lucky during the coming year.

From the ceiling suspend a large pumpkin, on whose rind all the letters of the alphabet have been burned or painted. Twirl this quickly and each guest in turn tries to stab some letter with a hatpin. The letter which is pierced is the initial letter of one's fate.

Another – swing a wedding ring over a goblet and repeat the alphabet slowly, the letter said as the ring touches the glass is the initial of the future wife or husband, as the case may be.

This same ring may be suspended from the ceiling, at a convenient distance from the floor. Whoever succeeds in running a pencil through it while walking towards it, without stopping, is the next to be married.

WATER CHARM.

Place three bowls on a table, one containing clear water, another soapy or muddy water, and the third one empty.

Blindfold the players one at a time, and lead them to the bowls, (whose positions are changed each time) to put their fingers in one of them.

If a player touches the clear water, he will be happily married; if the soapy water, he will marry a widow; and if he puts his finger in the empty bowl, he will never marry.

For knowing the occupation of the future one, there are several ways. Articles suggestive of different trades may be buried in flour, and the players in turn take a spoonful out of the dish and see what they can find. If not successful the first time, they may have a second trial.

Another way is to melt lead and then drop in into cold water, and the form it takes will suggest the trade of the future husband. Sometimes the forms are intricate, but if they suggest any trade, that is the real one. If it flattens out and looks like a book, an author will be the fate; if in tiny pieces, like particles of dirt, a farmer will be suggested, and so on.

OVER THE CIDER MUGS.

By each place at the table place a mug of sweet cider, a small bunch of matches, two candles, and a slip of paper with a pencil.

Before the refreshments are served, when all are seated, the hostess announces that as she counts twenty-five slowly, each guest is to write a wish on the paper, light a candle, burn the paper in the light, letting the ashes fall into the cider, and drink the contents of the mug, ashes and all. All who succeed in doing this before twenty-five is counted, will have their wishes granted.

Later, ask each guest to light both candles, naming each after a sweetheart, and allow them to burn as long as they will. The candle which burns longest shows which one will prove most faithful.

SHIPS OF FATE.

Prepare as many half-shells of walnuts as there are guests. In each fasten a small candle with a drop of the wax.

Fill a tub with water, and before sailing the boats, the water should be agitated so as to have it wavy. Two at a time may sail their boats, lighting the candles as they are launched. The life of the owner is prophesied by the seaworthy qualities of his ship.

If the storm overcomes the ship, the one whose it is, will be wrecked by adversity. The ship sailing across the tub signifies a long sea voyage, while those remaining by the side show that the person loves home better.

If the two ships stay together throughout the trip, the couple owning them will have a happy marriage. If they bump together, that signifies a quarrel, and if they sail in opposite directions, each person will lead a single life.

CAKE WITH CANDLES.

A large cake with as many different coloured candles on it as there are guests, is passed around, and each one takes a piece of it, with the candle too, choosing whatever colour they wish.

As the cake passes from one to the other, the hostess reads the following prophecies, having prepared them beforehand to suit the company:

Bright and cheery, candle red,
The year is here in which you wed.

If your candle green should be,
You will find your love at sea.

Lonely, hopeless, spinster she,
If white candle hers should be.

Happy he with candle blue,
Thy sweetheart is ever true.

She who holds a candle yellow,
Marries now a jealous fellow.

HUNT THE SQUIRREL.

To amuse the children after dinner, ask them all to join hands and form a ring. One is chosen out and is given a nut which he is to drop behind some child. As he walks around the outside of the ring he says:

> Hunt the squirrel in the woods,
> I lost him, I found him.
> Hunt the squirrel in the woods,
> I lost him, I found him.
> I won't catch you, and I won't catch you,
> But I will catch you.

As he says the last line, he drops the nut behind some child. That one must pick it up, and run around the circle, trying to reach his place before the other one gets there. If he fails, he is out and the game continues as before.

CHRISTMAS TREE.

A novel amusement for children at Christmas time is to trim a Christmas tree when blindfolded. Stand a small tree at one end of the room, ready to be trimmed. Have all the ornaments on a table near at hand, ready to be put on the tree.

Blindfold the children one at a time, lead them to the table to take their pick. The first thing touched must be taken, and after turning the child around three times start him straight toward the tree.

When he reaches the tree, he must wire the ornament, or whatever he had, in place. Some older person can be ready to turn the tree around, as it will be trimmed only on one side, if not. The children can have as many turns as they wish until the tree is trimmed.

CHRISTMAS GUESSES.

Suspend a large bunch of mistletoe from one of the chandeliers. The children, one at a time, stand under the mistletoe, and guess how many berries there are on it. The berries are counted when all have guessed. The one coming the nearest receives a prize.

While watching the Christmas tree, after the presents have been distributed, someone says, 'I see something on the Christmas tree which commences with T. What is it?' Many guesses are given, the one who says 'Tinsel', has guessed correctly, and it is his turn to give a guess, which may commence with P and C. PopCorn is easily guessed, and so on, until everything has been guessed.

CHRISTMAS WREATH.

Suspend a large Christmas wreath in a doorway at a convenient height from the floor. Prepare in advance 'snowballs', made of cotton batting covered with white tissue paper.

The players stand about eight feet from the wreath, and take turns, one at a time. Each is given three 'snowballs', and the one who succeeds in throwing all three, one at a time, through the wreath, is given the prize.

To make it more exciting, sides may be chosen, and each one of the three snowballs numbered, one being 5, the other, 10, and the third, 20. If the ball numbered 5 goes through, it counts 5 for that player's side. If it does not go through, it is a loss, and so on. The side scoring the most points is victorious.

CHRISTMAS CANDLES.

A small tree is placed on a table. The candles are lighted. Blindfold the players, one at a time, turn around three times, and allow each to take five steps toward the tree. Then he must blow as hard as he can, endeavouring to blow out all the lights, if possible. The one who succeeds in extinguishing the most receives a prize.

Another amusement is playing 'The Night Before Christmas' like 'Stagecoach'. Give each child the name of some part of Santa Claus' outfit, the sleigh, the reindeer, etc. The hostess then reads the well-known story, 'The Night Before Christmas.' As she mentions the names, the players having them, rise, turn around, and sit down again. When she mentions Santa Claus, all change places, and she tries to secure a seat. The one left out continues the story, and so on, until completed.

A GAME WITHIN A GAME.

While the children are waiting on Christmas for their presents, or dinner, or whenever the time seems to drag, suggest that each one think up the best game he knows.

Give each child a pencil and a card on which the game and the name of the child who thought of it are written. Each one in turn tells his game and all the children play it. When all have had a turn, and each game has been played, the children look over their lists and choose the game they liked best. The originator of the most popular one receives a prize.

TOSS THE GOODIES.

The children form a square, each one holding the sides of an old table-cloth or piece of sheeting. In the centre of this is placed a pile of nuts, candies, raisins, fruits, and all sorts of goodies. When a signal is given, the children all together toss the cloth up and down, singing:

Toss the goodies up and down,
Up and down, up and down,
Toss the goodies up and down,
Goodies for you and me.

When the last line is sung, an extra large toss is made and thus all the goodies fly to all parts of the room. The children then all scramble around picking them up and having a jolly time.

SNOWBALLS.

A pretty idea for concealing Christmas presents for the children is to make a lot of snowballs out of white tissue paper and cotton batting, and concerting the gifts inside.

Pile all these snowballs under the tree, and when the time comes for distributing them, the mother, or some older person tosses them, one at a time, to the children, who are standing at a distance eagerly waiting for them.

As the children catch them they step out of line to leave room for others until all have received one. Then all the balls are opened and the presents disclosed.

DECKING SANTA CLAUS.

Santa, who has been invited to the party, after being introduced to all the children, sits at the end of the room.

The children are blindfolded one at a time, and after being turned around three or four times, are told to walk up to him, and place on his head their own caps, which they had received in bonbons just before.

The child who succeeds in decking Santa Claus with his own cap may receive a little prize.